THE HUMANNESS OF HEROES

THE AMSTERDAM VERGIL LECTURES, VOLUME 1
general editor: David Rijser

This is the first of a series of monographs on Vergil based on lectures at the University of Amsterdam.

THE HUMANNESS
OF HEROES

Studies in the Conclusion of Virgil's *Aeneid*

Michael C. J. Putnam

MICHAEL C. J. PUTNAM

For Robert Stanton —
with the author's great affection —
Rockport — viii-10-12

AMSTERDAM UNIVERSITY PRESS

Cover design: Geert de Koning, Ten Post
Lay-out: Sander Pinkse Boekproductie, Amsterdam

ISBN   978 90 8964 347 6
e-ISBN 978 90 4851 482 3
NUR   617, 683

For David Rijser

Table of Contents

Preface

The following chapters were delivered as the University of Amsterdam Lectures on Virgil, given in November, 2009, at Amsterdam and Leiden, a series which I had the pleasure of inaugurating.

I thank Dr. David Rijser for his invitation to deliver the talks, for the ensuing challenge of formulating for an audience my most recent ideas on the end of the *Aeneid*, and for providing the occasion to rethink others that have been a part of my scholarly life for many decades. As befitted a superb student of Virgil, his introductions and summaries deftly led the listeners along a sometimes intricate path with verve, clarity, and elegance. As hosts, he and his wife, Dr. Jacqueline Klooster, were enthusiastic and untiring, making available to us the intellectual, artistic, and musical *richesse* of Amsterdam as well as a legion of colleagues, friends, and students who memorably enhanced our experience of a great city during our all too brief visit.

In the subsequent preparation of the lectures for publication, David Rijser has been the best of readers, generously sharing his own wisdom while suggesting ways to enhance my presentation. My debt to him is acknowledged on a separate page.

I would like also to thank in particular Professor Irene de Jong, whose combination of intelligence and warmth added greatly to the post-lecture periods of discussion as well as to the festive moments that surrounded the talks themselves. In Leiden, Professor Karl Enenkel provided a signal day, which began with the privilege of examining the Oblongus and Quadratus manuscripts of Lucretius and ended with a fine dinner at which he and his wife, Henriette van den Tooren, were hosts. I am also indebted to Professor Hans Smolenaars and his wife, Fanny Struyk, for a happy evening in Haarlem, where we were enthralled by Roman glass and the best of company. My thanks also to Stephen van Beek and Maurits de Leeuw for help in the book's final preparation.

On the other side of the pond I would like to thank Kenneth Gaulin for sharing with me this adventure along with many others. My students and colleagues at Brown, especially Mary Louise Gill, have been ever helpful. And once again I am grateful to my family for its unfailing support.

The epigraph to chapter 5 is excerpted from "Turnus," from *Departure:*

Since the following chapters were delivered as lectures, I have kept elaborate citations to a minimum in the notes. The enormous expanse of Virgilian studies would preclude more than a modest enumeration of references. To attempt a full list of scholarly writing devoted merely to the conclusion of Virgil's epic would be a daunting task whose feasibility would in any case lie beyond the scope of this slim volume. As partial substitute I have appended a bibliography of the most salient items that have influenced my work over the years. Within it I have included a selection of my own previous writing on the subject.

Michael C. J. Putnam
Cambridge, Massachusetts
July, 2011

Introduction

What can we see or acquire, but what we are? You have observed a skilful man reading Virgil. Well, that author is a thousand books to a thousand persons. Take the book into your hands, and read your eyes out; you will never find what I find.

Ralph Waldo Emerson, "Spiritual Laws," from *Essays: First Series*

There on brown Egina this light broke a Roman heart
Virgil's, whose voice comforts in our unlimited dark.

Edwin Denby, "Attica," from *Mediterranean Sonnets*

I N THE FOLLOWING LECTURES I will be offering a series of close critical readings of Virgil's *Aeneid*. My main project is to look at the epic's
human dimension, in particular at the unfolding of Aeneas's self-expres-
sion. Virgil never describes his protagonist directly. Rather, he asks of
us to appreciate the quality of his hero by means of the suggestiveness
of the narrative. Through the course of the epic the hero evolves from
an apparently stoical, self-effacing leader of his people, passive victim of
Juno's storm of jealous anger that opens the poem, burdened with the
founding of Rome and putting this destiny ahead of any personal desires,
into the fury-driven, vengeful conqueror who, his power now assured,
kills his humbled opponent at the conclusion of the poem.

As it should be to some degree for all readers, this ending and its possible meaning or meanings will be our primary focus. The final book itself
is a microcosm of the whole. Not only does it act as a superb finale, it
also serves as a resumé of the poem, drawing together the many strands
of thought and expression that anticipate the epic's conclusion and sup-
porting their force. Through its course we move from a calm Aeneas,
called *pius* according to his standard epithet, without his helmet, weaponless[1] and therefore vulnerable, asking for repression of the outburst of
anger subsequent to the breaking of the truce,[2] to the victor at the end
whose use of his weapons we now carefully observe. He first wounds his
opponent, Turnus, with a spear. Then in a rage he kills him with sword
buried into his chest — both deadly instruments now put to powerful
use. As point of contrast we will devote a lecture to the authority that
Virgil carefully bestows on Aeneas's defeated adversary in the poem's
concluding moments.

But our eyes will be mostly on Aeneas. Among other topics we will trace
the hero's ironic association with the literal, or figurative, destruction of
cities through the course of the poem. But chiefly we will watch how Virgil asks his reader to examine the various means by which earlier books
of the poem anticipate and sustain the power of its ending. The anger of
Juno at the start is recreated in the emotions of her earlier prey at the
poem's end, but already in book 2 Aeneas's own narration to Dido has us
contemplate him preparing to kill Helen in the position of suppliant.[3]

We will also examine, beginning in the chapters that immediately follow, the rampage on which Aeneas embarks in book 10 after the killing of his protégé Pallas — an intense bout of fury that is far disproportionate to the event that it claims to avenge. Virgil's words in describing it anticipate the final human sacrifice that the poet has us understand his hero is perpetrating in the epic's last moments.

Aeneas has been told by his father to spare the prideful once they have been battled down into the position of a suppliant.[4] Virgil carefully prepares us to view the final confrontation between the hero and his opponent as an archetypal example to test the possibility of enforcing this paternal injunction. Turnus has been apostrophized prominently by the narrator in book 10 as "you, proud Turnus" (*te, Turne, superbe*)[5] and he is at the epic's conclusion abased by his antagonist's force of arms. That Aeneas kills in a fury aroused by remembrance of Pallas instead of sparing his pleading foe by dispassionately adhering to the magnanimous clemency advocated by his father speaks to the truth of his humanity.

It also speaks to the conscience of his poet who would have us complete our reading of his masterpiece by focusing our thoughts on his hero's individuality. We do not end, no matter how much some critics would wish it so, anticipating some glorious future to come, with Aeneas portrayed as the model of regal decorum. In spite of Anchises's wish to the contrary, and whatever the poet's intent, Aeneas's behavior does not establish a pattern for moderation in the employment of power by Roman statesmen to follow. In fact, it does the opposite.

By focusing the reader's concentration on the hero's furious anger, Virgil has us return cyclically not only to the initial books of his own epic but to the start of the *Iliad* and to the wrath of Achilles, which is Homer's first, portentous word, paralleled in force by *arma* as the Roman poet's opening.[6] By means of this weighty abstraction and its elaborate deployment, Virgil deliberately inaugurates with his great predecessor a dialogue whose residue permeates the *Aeneid* and is to be discovered not least through the study of lexical usage, narrative strategies, and ethical values. It is on the latter that Aeneas's display of emotion at the end of his poem would have us particularly dwell.

We will return regularly to this point in the chapters that follow. But it is well to summarize here some salient differences between the two master poets. Virgil's epic ends with the equivalent of the events of the *Iliad's* twenty-second book, when Achilles kills Hector with revenge for the latter's slaying of Patroclus uppermost in his mind. In Homer there follow the funeral games for Patroclus, the ransoming of Hector by his father Priam, the city's ancient king, and the funeral and triple lamentations for the Trojan hero that bring the poem to a sad but satisfying close.

Virgil offers us none of these moments of emotional release and ca-
tharsis. We end with a violent death and with the slain hero's soul fleeing
resentfully beneath the shades. We also end with Aeneas as full-fledged
refiguration of Achilles, the vengeful, merciless killer of a suppliant Hector in the twenty-second book of the *Iliad*. It is Achilles who initiates
the downfall of Troy, an analogy that Virgil's suggestiveness urges us to
pursue from early moments in his epic on. As we will see in detail, Virgil would have us also draw a comparison between Aeneas and Achilles's
son, Pyrrhus, who kills defenseless Priam in one of the epic's most gruesome scenes.

I do not mean to imply that Achilles is more given to vengeance than
is Aeneas. Part of the challenge in dealing with the parallels between the
two heroes is the very complexity of their portrayals by Homer and Virgil. Achilles can withhold vengeance when he chooses, as at the *Iliad*'s
start. He is given to melancholy, loves poetry, and is strongly attached
to Briseis as well as to Patroclus. His interaction with Priam in the epic's
final book is profoundly moving. Nevertheless, where the correspond-
ence between both heroes reaches a climax, in book 22 of the *Iliad*, as
Achilles kills Hector, and at the conclusion of the *Aeneid*, at the death of
Turnus, it is upon the common propensity of the heroes for savage retaliation when they have been deeply aggrieved that each poet would have
us center our attention.[7]

We will take for granted the Augustan aspects of the poem, which appear most prominently at those moments when Virgil allows us to peer
far ahead and enjoy glimpses of Rome's golden age, initiated under its
first emperor. In this dream of a time to come, civil war is brought to
an end and the personified "unholy Madness" that sets brother against
brother, *impius Furor*,[8] is now chained in prison once the historic battle
off Actium has brought Rome's century of fraternal slaughter to an end.
But Virgil is a far greater poet than to press allegory into service in so
superficial a manner, which is to say to suggest some intense connection
between Aeneas and Augustus simply because the Trojan hero is the initial founder of a noble race and Rome's first emperor is a later restorer of
that same people to an age of unparalleled prosperity and calm founded
on the measured use of omnipotence.

What Virgil does in fact show us is something quite different for his
core narrative. The Trojans are in actuality treated as an invading army
taking on in battle those who are supposedly fated to be their future
brethren. And Aeneas, instead of sparing his defeated foe, kills him in
an outburst of passionate revenge, with fury on the loose, triumphant

instead of incarcerated. It is one of Virgil's richest ironies that the goddess he addresses at the start of his epic's second half is Erato,[9] a muse presumably serving to inspire the creation of poetry concerned with *eros*. Why does the poet choose a goddess associated with love to preside over six books of an epic nominally devoted to the transfer of empire from one continent to another and to doing battle to make that shift permanent in anticipation of a later, splendid history? It is a question that Virgil wishes his reader to ponder for the last half of his masterpiece and to which he suggests a plausible answer only in its concluding thirty lines. The *Aeneid*, we learn at last, is a poem that is concerned as much with the complexities of love as of war.

This leads me to suggest, as I will again in the Epilogue, that there are crucial parallels between Aeneas and Augustus which are multiform. Just as the complementarity between Aeneas and Achilles can be viewed from many angles, so the connection between Virgil's hero and the ruler of Rome during his time of writing is far from simple. The poem, as I attempt to illustrate, should not be reduced to the status of a one-dimensional panegyric, however much the glory of future Rome surfaces during its narrative.

Both Aeneas and Augustus need to resort to violence as they go about their careers — Aeneas in the establishment of a new foundation and in the securing of its integrity, Augustus in assuring his own position of authority as a bringer of peace and a renewer of wholeness to the Roman world after a century of civil strife. In so doing both reveal less attractive sides of their natures as they are forced by complicated circumstances to acts of injustice though their dispositions might be equally prone to pity and reconciliation.

It is Virgil's greatest compliment to his ruler that he makes no attempt to minimize or even to gloss over the faults of Aeneas any more than he does, vicariously, the flaws of Augustus. There is in fact a deep parallelism between the poem's hero and the ruler of Rome, but it is one as complex as it is astute. The *Aeneid* is not a eulogy of Aeneas, Augustus or Rome, but in telling the truth about man's essentially unchanging character, whether seen through the lens of myth or apprised from the interpretation of historical events, Virgil pays the most genuine form of tribute his imagination could offer by his realistic, honest appraisal of the city's present as mirrored in its past.

At least in the case of Virgil, my sense is that the author himself, and not any particular theoretical model, offers the reader the most creative help in elucidating his text. Such is Virgil's mastery that verbal echoes draw our attention from one context to another. Their presence does not exemplify his virtuosity in modulating a repetitiveness stemming from his inheritance of the Homeric formula as a standard device of epic narrative. Rather, for Virgil they suggest a studied development of typologies throughout the poem, many of which reach a climax in its brilliant final book.

As a devotee of careful reading, my attention is regularly directed to a close examination of Virgil's lexicon, to his special use of words and to the nuanced meanings that he gives them. Figures of speech will also hold our attention and I allow my explications to devolve from the enriching study of figuration. For instance, we will trace the importance of similes as expansive metaphorical aids toward explaining the meaning of the texts that they ornament. We will examine individual similes as we move from book to book, but we will look particularly at how certain motifs established by discrete similes earlier in the epic reach a series of culminations in book 12.

Let us look at some examples. The previous parallelisms that Virgil draws between Aeneas and either a hunter or a shepherd are dramatically developed in book 12. Deer and dog, separated before in figuration or in story line, also unite now in a simile where Aeneas by himself is, for the first time in the poem, compared to an animal, a hunter hound pursuing Turnus, a frightened deer. Earlier similes devoted to bees likewise reach a climax at the end. In book 1 the Carthaginians embellishing their city are compared to artisan-bees going about their work of making honey, and in book 6 souls soon to be reborn from drinking at the fountain of Lethe are likened to bees buzzing around summer flowers. Their final appearance in the poem merges with Aeneas's last analogy to a shepherd when, as he gratuitously sets fire to Latinus's city, he is compared to a shepherd smoking out bees from their lair. Virgil tells us of smoke emerging as a result of the shepherd's deadly preoccupation, but nothing of bees. We have come a long way, and on a road with several scenic detours, from the Aeneas who in the second book in the midst of Troy's dark night of ruin compares himself, in his narrative to Dido, to an ignorant shepherd who passively, helplessly, listens as wind-driven fire or mountain torrent destroy the crops and landscape that stand for the civilization of the Trojan world.

As an axiom, I believe that pursuing the poet's words themselves is the best means to explain the complexity of this extraordinary poem, with one passage commenting upon another. In other words, and as a result, we will often be reading Virgil, as I said, with what aid we can garner from Virgil himself. For instance, in book 10, at a crucial moment to help us understand the poem's ending, Pallas, Aeneas's young charge, is said to be *sinistro / adfixus lateri*[10] ("affixed to [the older hero's] left side") as they descend the Tiber by boat from Pallanteum. The participle *adfixus* is usually translated through some locution suggesting nearness, e.g., "staying close" (Fairclough-Goold, Lombardo), "stayed close" (Day Lewis), "clings close" (Mandelbaum), "sticks close" (Ahl), "flanks him closely" (Fagles). But Virgil's use of the verb *adfixit* elsewhere is associated with a torch pierced into the side of a wooden tower (*Aen.* 9. 536), and we find *infixa* of a fatal arrow puncturing the side of a dying warrior (*Aen.* 9. 579). The poet's use of compounds of *figo* in these instances thus suggests that Pallas's presence next to Aeneas will have the metaphoric effect of a torch or an arrow, setting aflame or wounding that to which it is stuck. The emotional affect this proximity exerts on Aeneas is soon exhibited in his excessive reaction to Pallas's death, in the violent, vengeful course of slaughter on which he embarks, and in the final, furious killing of his killer, Turnus, when he has been pronouncedly reminded of that earlier death. We will begin in the first two chapters by an examination in detail of that earlier moment.

Two points at the start. First, throughout the pages that follow I will be striving to appreciate the ethics of the hero's behavior by the standards that the poem itself sets, not by any non-Virgilian criteria, whether ancient or modern. Secondly, how Augustus, and Augustan Rome, might have reacted to the particular forms of violence that are manifested in the narrative reflection of the *Aeneid* and in the behavior of its hero, especially in its concluding lines, is a subject that I will speculate upon in the Epilogue.

CHAPTER 1

The Rampage of Book 10: Part 1

KING: Then every soldier kill his prisoners!
Give the word through.

Shakespeare, *Henry V*, Act IV, Scene 6

KING: Besides, we'll cut the throats of those we have:
And not a man of them, that we shall take,
Shall taste our mercy. Go and tell them so.

Shakespeare, *Henry V*, Act IV, Scene 7

L ET US PLUNGE *in medias res.* I want to look closely at the lines in book 10 of our epic where for the first time Virgil begins to draw in detail the analogy between Aeneas and Achilles. The description of the shield of Aeneas in book 8 has already urged the reader to ponder the equivalent moment in *Iliad* 18 where the Greek hero receives his extraordinary armor. But only from the tenth book until the end of the epic does the poet draw out the connections in detail.[11]

We might briefly note some of the discrepancies that result from this analogy. The *Aeneid* tells the story of an expatriate Trojan prince who by the poem's end has, through war, established his power in Latium and, as Virgil points us toward time beyond his narrative, seems to emerge as the progenitor of Rome and a prefiguration, as it were, of its refounder, Augustus. At the start of the poem we empathize with the enduring Aeneas, tossed about on the storm of Juno's anger, Aeneas who, in book 2, becomes the symbol of filial piety for bearing his father, household gods in hand, and leading his son, out of the wreckage of Troy. Earlier in the same book Venus had reminded her son, after he had contemplated the killing of Helen, of the uselessness of furious, personal revenge by contrast with the pious necessity of caring for his family and of facing the destiny that this entails.

The second half of the epic complicates an already complex intersection. The Trojans turn from passive to active as their fate unfolds. From the endurers of exile and years of wandering they become the conquering invaders who also provoke that most Roman of misfortunes, an engagement with the enemy that initiates a very Roman pattern of civil warring.

I would like first to ask a question that focuses on one important aspect of how Virgil portrays this change. What does it mean for our understanding of Aeneas and his poem that, as the epic draws to its climax and conclusion, the poet is at pains to establish the parallelism of his hero with Achilles, semi-divine leader of the victorious Greeks, killer of Hector, the leading Trojan warrior, as an act of particular, personal vengeance for the death of his friend Patroclus, and in the end receiver of the suppliant Priam who comes to ransom his son Hector's corpse? I will maintain that the flash of human feeling that engulfs the hero at the epic's end complements, contradicts, and, in the poem's finale, supplants the quasi-impersonal structuring of conquest and empire, both in the present and in the future, that the epic has so elaborately established.

In book 6 Anchises carefully spells out to his son the ethics of forbearance, of the restrained use of power, especially against the haughty in defeat, that should set a pattern for Roman martial behavior to come and should serve, in particular, as a model for Caesar and Pompey and therefore for the future leaders of the Empire. The lines are familiar. "O Roman", says Aeneas's father, "remember to establish a custom for peace" (6. 853):

> '...parcere subiectis et debellare superbos.'

> "...to spare the humbled and war down the proud."[12]

In the epic's final books we watch as Virgil tests the piety that Aeneas owes his father's ethics of restraint against other emotional forces, among them what we might call the *pietas* of vengeance.

Virgil establishes the paradigm for this second example of loyalty in the lines that follow upon Aeneas's learning of the death of Pallas (10. 513–17). It is purposeful on Virgil's part that the occasion motivates the most brutal display of murderous force in the poem, extraordinary in particular because the poem's hero is its perpetrator:

> proxima quaeque metit gladio latumque per agmen
> ardens limitem agit ferro, te, Turne, superbum
> caede nova quaerens. Pallas, Evander, in ipsis
> omnia sunt oculis, mensae quas advena primas
> tunc adiit, dextraeque datae.

> With his sword he mows down whatever is nearby, and with the blade fiercely drives a broad path through the host, seeking you, Turnus, proud from your fresh slaughter. Pallas, Evander, everything is before his eyes, the meals that he then first came to as a stranger, the right hands proffered.

This is the clearest occasion where Virgil establishes Turnus as a figure for *superbia* (and hence as an exemplum of the prideful who, in Anchises's dictum, should be beaten down but spared).[13] And, as we saw, the poet makes the occasion telling for the reader by his use of apostrophe that serves verbally to incarnate Turnus before us as he is also actualized for Aeneas. And this same visual immediacy continues on as we enter the mind's eye of Aeneas, remembering his history with Evander and his young son whom Turnus has just killed. The universality of his destructiveness is echoed in the universality (*omnia*) of what he remembers from the events at Pallanteum. This parallelism, as I earlier suggested, helps configure a paradigm of commitment based on revenge. Evander's words at Pallas's funeral put the definition succinctly (11. 177–79):

> 'quod vitam moror invisam Pallante perempto
> dextera causa tua est, Turnum gnatoque patrique
> quam debere vides...'

> "The reason that I linger in this hated life now that Pallas has been slain is your right hand which you see owes Turnus to son and to father."

Aeneas's "seeing" is again crucial as Virgil melds the right hands exchanged in compact with Aeneas's right hand that now wields the sword-blade of power. We will focus on that same hand again, most prominently as the epic ends, when, for a moment of hesitation, of thought instead of action, the hero "checked his right hand" (*dextram...repressit*, 12. 939).[14]

But there is another element in this mix that complicates further any interpretation of Aeneas's behavior. To illustrate this, we must turn to allusion and to the specific lexical usage of poets. Line 513 of book 10 contains Virgil's only use of the verb *metere*, to reap. The metaphor of death-dealing warriors as harvesters in the midst of battle's bloodshed is as old as Homer,[15] but, as Oliver Lyne points out,[16] Virgil's unique usage points to Catullus and, in particular, to a passage in the earlier poet that refers to Achilles (64. 353–55):

> namque velut densas praecerpens messor aristas
> sole sub ardenti flaventia demetit arva,
> Troiugenum infesto prosternet corpora ferro.

> For just as a reaper, cutting the thick ears of grain, mows down the tawny fields under a burning sun, so he will lay low the bodies of the Trojans with his hostile sword-blade.

Since these are the only uses of *messor* and *demetit* in Catullus, they serve to secure the connection between the two passages.[17] The image of reaping that Homer employs in *Iliad* 11 to depict the general butchery as the Trojans and Achaeans slaughter each other, in Catullus becomes centralized specifically on the savagery of Achilles. Furthermore Achilles, in the larger context of poem 64, emerges as a symbol not only of one hero's barbaric conduct but also of the decadence of humankind in general, a negative force of nature associated, in line 354, with the burning heat of the summer sun in which the reaper works. We move from the golden moment of the wedding of Peleus and Thetis, when gods and mortals celebrated together, to a decline in civilization typified by Achilles's mercilessness on the battlefield, which in turn stands as prototype for a breakdown in standards in the ethics of man's behavior to man.[18]

I am suggesting that unique lexical usage in both poets takes us from Catullus's Achilles to Virgil's Aeneas, and, further, that the brutality of one hero, in the earlier context, is absorbed by the other, as the Augustan poet thinks back to the poem of his predecessor that was most influential on his writing of the *Aeneid*. This suggestion is confirmed by what follows in each poet. After the intervention of one intercalary line, Catullus offers us an illustration of the results of the heroism of Achilles (64. 357–60):

> testis erit magnis virtutibus unda Scamandri
> quae passim rapido diffunditur Hellesponto,
> cuius iter caesis angustans corporum acervis
> alta tepefaciet permixta flumina caede.

Witness to his great virtues will be the wave of the Scamander that pours itself abroad in the rushing Hellespont. Narrowing its course with stacks of slaughtered corpses, he will warm its deep streams with a mingling of slaughter.

In Virgil we turn to the first extraordinary act in the spate of ferocity on which Aeneas now embarks (*Aen.* 10. 517–20), parallel to the behavior of Achilles in *Iliad* 18 and 21:[19]

> Sulmone creatos
> quattuor hic iuvenes, totidem quos educat Ufens,
> viventis rapit, inferias quos immolet umbris
> captivoque rogi perfundat sanguine flammas.

Then he takes alive four youths, offspring of Sulmo, and the same number whom Ufens rears, whom he might sacrifice as offerings to the shades and bathe the flames with captive blood.

We hear of the victims again in book 11 where they form part of Pallas's funeral procession. The language is a careful recapitulation (81–82):

> vinxerat et post terga manus, quos mitteret umbris
> inferias, caeso sparsurus sanguine flammas,...

He had also bound behind their backs the hands of those whom he might send as offerings to the shades, sprinkling the flames with slaughtered blood.

It is not only metaphor that links Aeneas with Achilles, but narrative parallels as well. In giving pride of place in his catalogue of Aeneas's acts of bloodshed to the taking of human victims for sacrifice, Virgil directly links him to the Greek hero at his most savage.

We first hear of Achilles's plans at *Iliad* 18. 336–37, as he addresses the dead Patroclus:

> "...and of twelve glorious sons of the Trojans will I cut the throats before your pyre in my anger at your slaying."

Their actual capture occurs at 21. 26–32, in the midst of the Scamander:

> And he, when his hands grew weary from his slaughter, chose twelve youths alive from the river as blood-price for dead Patroclus, son of Menoetius. (26–28)

In book 23 we are twice told of their death. The first occasion comes as Achilles once again speaks to Patroclus in lamentation (22–23):[20]

> ...and of twelve glorious offspring of the Trojans would I cut the throats before your pyre in my anger at your slaying.

And their death scene concludes the sequence, first with narration (175–77):

> ...and he slew with the bronze twelve stalwart sons of the great-souled Trojans, for he pondered evil deeds in his heart, and he set the iron might of fire to consume them....

then with Achilles apostrophizing Patroclus (179–82):

> "Hail, O Patroclus, even in the house of Hades, for I now bring to pass everything that I promised earlier. Twelve stalwart sons of the great-souled Trojans, all these the flame devours along with you...."

But it is the actual moment of capture in *Iliad* 21 that is foremost in Virgil's mind and that therefore is essential for us to ponder. Catullus helps us make the transition from Achilles, the grim reaper, to the scene in the Scamander, clogged with the bodies of his victims. But it is Homer himself who supplies the particularities not only of Achilles's massacre in the river but of the seizure of the captives for later sacrifice. In sum, Virgil depicts Aeneas as having the killing of Pallas and his further allegiance to Evander in mind as he begins his rampage, but by lexical usage and allusion he asks of the reader to remember Achilles in Catullus and then in Homer and, as a result, to see in Aeneas an image of the Greek hero at his most vindictive.[21]

There are further details in Virgil's account to which we should attend, but which differentiate it from his model in Homer. One is the specificity of naming. The Trojan captives are anonymous. Virgil, by contrast, has us note the detailing of fathers and sons, and the family relationship is given special poignancy by the use of the present tense of *educat* (518), as if the rearing of the youths was still an on-going process. Another is the emphasis on blood. A human sacrifice is in the offing, and it is especially graphic that we hear first of captive blood, then of slaughtered blood. The enallage makes the reference notably forceful: it is the sons of Sulmo and Ufens who are being captured (in book 10) and then readied for slaughter (in book 11), but it is on their sacrificial blood that Virgil's figuration makes us attend, and not just on the victims themselves.

Another point of differentiation between Virgil and Homer is the number of victims seized by each hero. In Homer it is twelve, in Virgil eight. And in this instance, as we turn back to the masterpiece that precedes the *Aeneid*, it is Virgil himself who can help explain to us his choice of number. As the fourth book of the *Georgics* comes to a conclusion, Aristaeus, who has lost his bees, learns that he must offer a sacrifice of appeasement to the dead Eurydice and her fellow nymphs. The result of the successful completion of this ceremony will be the restoration of his hive. First we learn from Cyrene, Aristaeus's mother, of the rubrics to be followed (4. 537–43):

> 'sed modus orandi qui sit prius ordine dicam:
> quattuor eximios praestanti corpore tauros,
> qui tibi nunc viridis depascunt summa Lycaei,

delige, et intacta totidem cervice iuvencas.
quattuor his aras alta ad delubra dearum
constitue, et sacrum iugulis demitte cruorem,
corporaque ipsa boum frondoso desere luco.'

"But first I will tell you in order the manner of your supplication. Pick out four choice bulls, of surpassing form, that now graze among your herds on the heights of green Lycaeus, and as many heifers of unyoked neck. For these set up four altars by the stately shrines of the goddesses, and drain the sacrificial blood from their throats, but leave the bodies of the steers within the leafy grove."(Fairclough-Goold)

The gist of the goddess's instructions is repeated by the narrator shortly later as Aristaeus implements them (549–51):

ad delubra venit, monstratas excitat aras,
quattuor eximios praestanti corpore tauros
ducit et intacta totidem cervice iuvencas.

He comes to the shrine, raises the altars appointed, and leads there four choice bulls, of surpassing form, and as many heifers of unyoked neck.

Through both the number (eight) of victims involved and the phraseology of their count (*quattuor...totidem*), in one case male and female cattle, in the other, two groups of sons, each set with different fathers, Virgil leads us to draw an analogy between the two ceremonies. The comparison emphasizes the gruesomeness of Aeneas's actions in book 10. On a general level and in an ugly worsening of ethical values, humans, in their position as part of a family chain, replace beautiful, unbroken animals as the sacrificial offerings. Moreover, whereas productive good comes for Aristaeus in his regained liaison with the gods and in the restoration of his bees, nothing palpably creative results from Aeneas's anger, only his presumed inner satisfaction at the realization of his desire for vengeance.[22] This occurs in a way that, as we have seen, aligns him with Achilles at the moral low point of his behavior (we remember that even Homer calls his hero's deed evil).

One more detail both links the two sacrifices and further underlines the horror of Aeneas's action vis-à-vis that of Achilles. Here again blood is involved. Achilles merely seizes his prisoners and burns them on the pyre, along with the body of his friend. Aeneas, we learn twice from the narration, takes his prey so that he can bathe or sprinkle the pyre of Pallas with blood. Virgil tells us nothing about casting the bodies into the fire, only that blood will be poured onto the flames. This suggests that the captives were first killed, then drained of blood, which was subsequently used to drench the pyre.[23] The detail is a grisly addition to what Homer tells us of Achilles, and it increases our revulsion at Aeneas-Achilles, especially when his deed is seen against the standard of self-control and restraint that both his father and his mother have set for him. If such action exemplifies the *pietas* of revenge, it is not displayed for the reader in a positive light.

The same tonality persists in the next episode. Here Homer alone provides the transition from scene to scene. The confrontation of Lycaon with Achilles, which follows immediately upon his selecting for sacrifice the Trojan youths from the river, also offered Virgil the model, in general and in particular details,[24] for Aeneas's dealings with Magus in the event subsequent to his seizing of the young Latins (10. 521–36):

> inde Mago procul infensam contenderat hastam:
> ille astu subit, at tremibunda supervolat hasta,
> et genua amplectens effatur talia supplex:
> 'per patrios manis et spes surgentis Iuli
> te precor, hanc animam serves gnatoque patrique.
> est domus alta, iacent penitus defossa talenta
> caelati argenti, sunt auri pondera facti
> infectique mihi. non hic victoria Teucrum
> vertitur aut anima una dabit discrimina tanta.'
> dixerat. Aeneas contra cui talia reddit:
> 'argenti atque auri memoras quae multa talenta
> gnatis parce tuis. belli commercia Turnus
> sustulit ista prior iam tum Pallante perempto.
> hoc patris Anchisae manes, hoc sentit Iulus.'
> sic fatus galeam laeva tenet atque reflexa
> cervice orantis capulo tenus applicat ensem.

Next at Magus from a distance he had aimed the hostile lance. Deftly he cowers — the lance flies quivering over him — and, clasping the hero's knees, he speaks thus in supplication: "By the spirit of your father, by your hope in growing Iulus, I entreat you, save my life for a son and for a father. I have a lofty house; buried deep inside lie talents of chased silver, and I have masses of gold, wrought and unwrought. Not on me does the victory of Troy turn, nor will one life make a difference so great." He spoke, and Aeneas thus replied: "Those many talents of silver and gold that you tell of, keep them for your sons. Such trafficking in war Turnus put away before now, even at the time when Pallas was slain. Thus judges my father Anchises's spirit, thus Iulus." So speaking he grasps the helmet with his left hand and, bending back the suppliant's neck, drives the sword in up to the hilt. (Fairclough-Goold)

Virgil draws much from the Homeric episode. In both scenes the successful hero's spear passes over the head of his foe, who clasps his conqueror's knees in supplication. The outcome of each revolves on the notion of ransom and therefore on the possibility of victor sparing the defeated man who prays for mercy. In both situations the petition is denied. Here is Achilles speaking (*Il.* 21. 99–103):

> "Fool, do not offer me ransom or make speeches. Until Patroclus met his day of destiny, then it was more pleasant to my soul to spare the Trojans and many I took alive and sold into slavery. But now there is none that will escape death...."

The larger scope of Achilles's practice of sparing, changed now at the death of Patroclus, is narrowed in the case of Aeneas, given to lack of clemency because of a particular deed, Turnus's killing of Pallas.

But there are deeper resonances to Virgil's narrative than the parallels with Homer suggest. Let us look briefly at a few. Take the phrase *genua amplectens* (523), for instance. The only other instance in the *Aeneid* where *genua* is used with a form of *amplector* is at 3. 607, where the Greek Achaemenides, abandoned by Ulysses, appeals to Aeneas for mercy:

> 'dixerat et genua amplexus genibusque volutans
> haerebat...'

> "He spoke, and clasping our knees, grovelling at our knees, he clung to us..." (Williams)

It is Anchises, not Aeneas, who sets the pattern for *clementia* in the action of the epic by shortly thereafter offering the Greek suppliant his right hand in friendship.[25]

Anchises also twice enters our thoughts in Magus's opening words:

'per patrios manis et spes surgentis Iuli
te precor, hanc animam serves gnatoque patrique.'

He is named explicitly by Aeneas at 534 as the episode comes full circle:

'hoc patris Anchisae manes, hoc sentit Iulus.'

We think of him twice, first through his naming, secondly because Virgil's words take us back to a pivotal moment when the epic's hero is himself a suppliant. Aeneas is praying to the Sibyl for help in visiting his father in the Underworld (*Aen.* 6. 115–17):

'quin, ut te supplex peterem et tua limina adirem
idem orans mandata dabat. gnatique patrisque,
alma, precor, miserere....'

"Indeed he himself in prayer gave me orders as a suppliant to seek you out and to approach your threshold. Gracious one, I pray you, have pity on both son and father...."

The double reference to Anchises, by direct mention and by allusion, is of special importance for helping us gauge the appropriateness of Aeneas's conduct toward Magus.[26] Because his prayer to the Sibyl is successful, son can visit father and receive, at the climax of their conversation, Anchises's essential dictum about sparing suppliants. Virgil's allusiveness therefore pits Aeneas's surface violence, based on what I have been designating the *pietas* of vengeance, against the reader's understanding of what should be his ethical benchmark. Homer may serve as the model for the episode itself and for the Achillean behavior that its hero demonstrates during it, but Virgil carefully has his reader think back to Anchises — his deeds in book 3, his words in book 6 — and to the major difference in the ethos of power between the ethical environment that the Roman poet creates and that of Homer's *Iliad*. Through Anchises Virgil raises the moral stakes for Roman martial behavior, but, here at least, Homer and Achilles set the ruling pattern.

Finally I would like to turn to the last detail of the episode:

sic fatus galeam laeva tenet atque reflexa
cervice orantis capulo tenus applicat ensem.

The only other use in the *Aeneid* of the phrase *capulo tenus* is at 2. 553, where Pyrrhus kills Priam.[27] I quote the whole context that describes what follows after a speech by Achilles's son to the old king (550–53):

> '...hoc dicens altaria ad ipsa trementem
> traxit et in multo lapsantem sanguine nati,
> implicuitque comam laeva, dextraque coruscum
> extulit ac lateri capulo tenus abdidit ensem.'

> "Saying this he dragged him, trembling and slipping in his son's out-pouring of blood, to the very altar, and he entwined his left hand in his hair, and with his right drew forth the gleaming sword and buried it up to the hilt in his side."

The allusion increases the horror of the situation in the Magus episode, at its conclusion and climax. Aeneas now becomes not only Achilles, but his son Pyrrhus, remembered at one of the ugliest moments in the poem as the young warrior kills Troy's ancient ruler in a particularly ghastly manner, with sword to its full extent thrust through body.

The setting is important. Priam is at the altar,[28] the place where the act of supplication is most to be respected. Moreover, after Pyrrhus has killed Polites in front of his father and now prepares to kill the father himself, Virgil (through Aeneas's words) has Priam remind his enemy of another act of supplication in the past of both protagonists (2. 540–43):

> 'at non ille, satum quo te mentiris, Achilles
> talis in hoste fuit Priamo; sed iura fidemque
> supplicis erubuit corpusque exsangue sepulcro
> reddidit Hectoreum meque in mea regna remisit.'

> "But that Achilles, by whom you lie that you were fathered, was not such toward his enemy Priam, but he respected the rights and trust of a suppliant and gave back Hector's bloodless corpse for burial and sent me back to my kingdom."

By having Aeneas assume the posture of Pyrrhus at the end of the Magus episode, Virgil reminds us, first, of the Greek killing of a helpless old man at a suppliant's altar. But he also has us ponder, through Priam's words, the fact that Achilles had once respected the king's prayer and accepted ransom for the body of Hector.

Therefore, as Aeneas becomes a Pyrrhus figure at the end of the episode, he is made to outdo in brutality the evils of Pyrrhus's father by adopting the position of the son who makes such a prominent appearance in book 2. Though Achilles had killed Hector, he at least later respected Priam's posture of suppliant and accepted his ransom for the hero's corpse.[29] Aeneas-Pyrrhus both spurns a suppliant along with his offer of ransom and kills him in a particularly graphic manner.[30] So, though the theme of suppliancy runs through the episode, Aeneas himself is made to change in its course from Homer's Achilles of *Iliad* 21 to Virgil's Pyrrhus of *Aeneid* 2. It is a change that deepens the moral darkness into which his roles as reaper of the bodies of his enemies and seizer of human captives for sacrifice have already plunged him. The reader, meanwhile, through Virgil's brilliant artistry, is made also yet again to see his behavior against the backdrop of Anchises's demands for temperateness in the treatment of the defeated, suppliant foe.[31]

To conclude, Virgil poises us, and his hero, between two modes of *pietas* whose mutual incompatibility spills over into the contradictory ways in which the poet has us see Aeneas. These contradictions surface again in their most forceful presentation at the poem's end, where Aeneas kills, for the last and most powerful time, an antagonist who is also now a suppliant.[32] The action of the hero, "set aflame by furies and frightening in his wrath," may find him in the throes of the piety of vendetta and revenge. But shortly before he kills, Aeneas has been reminded of Anchises by his pleading foe just as on several levels the reader is made to think of Aeneas's father, and his authoritative utterances, during the Magus episode. It is his patriarch's words commanding emotional constraint that in both instances work in extraordinary, idealizing counterpoint to the more human anger which goads him to perform the two acts of killing a suppliant. One, as we have seen, comes in the midst of a spate of barbaric behavior. The other brings the poem to its powerful, perhaps contradictory, certainly paradoxical conclusion.

In the next chapter we will continue and conclude our examination of the narrative of Aeneas's spate of killing after the death of Pallas.

CHAPTER 2

The Rampage of Aeneas: Part 2

TITUS: What, villain boy,
Barr'st me my way in Rome?
He attacks Mutius
MUTIUS: Help, Lucius, help!
He kills him

Shakespeare, *Titus Andronicus*, Act I, Scene 1

ANY DIRECT PARALLEL with Achilles is absent from the next two segments of Aeneas's rampage, but Virgil develops motifs from the preceding episodes and adds new ones. The first is devoted to Haemonides (10. 537–42)

> nec procul Haemonides, Phoebi Triviaeque sacerdos,
> infula cui sacra redimibat tempora vitta,
> totus conlucens veste atque insignibus albis.
> quem congressus agit campo, lapsumque superstans
> immolat ingentique umbra tegit, arma Serestus
> lecta refert umeris tibi, rex Gradive, tropaeum.

Close by was Haemon's son, priest of Phoebus and Trivia, his temples wreathed in the fillet's sacred band, all glittering in his white robe and armor. Him Aeneas meets and drives over the plain; then bestriding the fallen man, he slaughters him and wraps him in mighty darkness; Serestus gathers his armor and carries away on his shoulders, a trophy, king Gradivus, for you!

Virgil here offers two striking reminders of what had gone before. Haemonides's role as "priest of Phoebus and Trivia" (*Phoebi Triviaeque sacerdos*) serves in part the same purpose as the phrase *gnatoque patrique* in the previous vignette. It recalls the position of the Sibyl as likewise *Phoebi Triviaeque sacerdos* (6. 35). In so doing, it prompts the reader once again to remember an earlier Aeneas, pleading for the priestess's help in visiting his father with all that this encounter will imply for his future behavior. It is vicious enough to kill a priest, but Virgil adds to the moral outrage by having us think of the particular importance of the Sibyl's role as crucial mediator between son and father, and between the worlds of the living and of the dead, documenting the most formidable act of *pietas* in the poem.[33]

The word *immolat*, especially through its reflection of the preceding example of *immolet* (519), also continues the notion of human sacrifice that the initial episode had adumbrated. But now a further irony is added. The priest who should ordinarily be the sacrificant is, by Aeneas's action and through the poet's lexicon, put in the place of the victim, and the hero becomes himself a macabre officiant, sacrificing a human offering who, like the sons of Sulmo and Ufens, serves to replace — and, in our thoughts, to become — the animal victim who would regularly be the priest's oblation.

We also notice the energy that Aeneas puts into his pursuit (*agit campo*) and the position he takes over the fallen (*superstans*). Since this is Virgil's only use of *supersto*, the reader gives the verb special attention and therefore watches closely Aeneas's posture of "standing over" his fallen foe — a pose akin to that of Turnus, whom not much earlier we had seen as *superbum* (10. 514). Aeneas, too, has his hauteur, and never spares suppliants, even priests as suppliants, neither here nor elsewhere.

In this respect also Aeneas is akin to Achilles who, in *Iliad* 22, fails to spare the defeated Hector though he pleads for mercy. It is Homer's forceful narrative that Virgil draws upon for an exemplum that Aeneas will emulate. The abstract *dicta* of Anchises, expounding a novel morality for Aeneas and future Romans to follow, are not allowed by Virgil to enter the thinking of his hero as he prepares to act.

Finally we should note the striping of Haemonides's armor to form a *tropaeum*. The warrior must be killed in order to be refashioned, in a grotesque version of synecdoche, into a body-shaped tree-trophy that memorializes both death and victory.[34] When Aeneas manufactures his Mezentius-trophy at the beginning of book 11, he calls the results of his artistry *primitiae* (11. 16), a corrupt, grim presentation of a human war-prize in place of the first-fruits of crops to celebrate the initial fertility of the agricultural year.[35] His sacrifice of Haemonides prepares the way for the later, more expansive version of Aeneas as the offerer of hideous presents to a god. Here, first, the benefaction is a slain hero metamorphosed into an armor-bearing tree trunk, not the usual grain, and, as in the later case of Mezentius, it is Mars, not Ceres, who serves as the appropriate receiver of his novel gift of a priest himself, not of what a sacrificant would ordinarily present to his divine protector.[36]

There follows the second non-Achillean episode (543–49):

> Instaurant acies Volcani stirpe creatus
> Caeculus et veniens Marsorum montibus Umbro.
> Dardanides contra furit: Anxuris ense sinistram
> Et totum clipei ferro deiecerat orbem
> (dixerat ille aliquid magnum vimque adfore verbo

crediderat, caeloque animum fortasse ferebat
canitiemque sibi et longos promiserat annos)....

Caeculus, born of Vulcan's race, and Umbro, who comes from the Marsian hills, repair the ranks. The offspring of Dardanus rages against them. With his sword he had felled the left hand of Anxur to the ground and the whole circle of his shield (he had uttered something mighty and had thought that force would attend his word, and was perhaps raising his spirit to heaven and had promised himself old age and length of years)....

Anxur is not mentioned elsewhere in the poem, though we presume that he is the eponymous establisher of the town of the same name on the Latian coast south of Rome. We have already been introduced to Caeculus during the catalogue of Latin allies of Turnus (7. 678–90) as the "founder of the city of Praeneste"[37] (*Praenestinae fundator...urbis*, 678). So, for the first and maybe the second time Virgil has Aeneas direct his rage against an Italian leader who is the architect of a city as well. It happens that this is also the first occasion where Virgil calls Aeneas Dardanides, descendant of Dardanus. In this context the patronymic is a clear reminder of Dardanus's supposed birth at Corythus, modern Cortona, in Etruria.[38] Thus the precursor-originator of Rome, Trojan offshoot of an Italian forbear, is now in the process of killing his Italian opponents, one of whom at least has been graphically presented to us as the immediate establisher of a city.[39] We are watching a conflict between founders that helps to confirm the pattern of a civil war in process.

Mention of Umbro furthers these implications. He, too, appears in the list of Latin allies in book 7 and, though he comes as emissary of King Archippus from Marruvium, the principal town of the Marsi, his name suggests that he represents the province of Umbria itself as he confronts his raging opponent and, like Caeculus, is also killed.[40] But Virgil would have us ponder other aspects of his presence. I quote the whole of his entry in the catalogue (7. 750–60):

Quin et Marruvia venit de gente sacerdos
fronde super galeam et felici comptus oliva
Archippi regis missu, fortissimus Umbro,
vipereo generi et graviter spirantibus hydris
spargere qui somnos cantuque manuque solebat,
mulcebatque iras et morsus arte levabat.
sed non Dardaniae medicari cuspidis ictum

evaluit neque eum iuvere in vulnera cantus
somniferi et Marsis quaesitae montibus herbae.
te nemus Angitiae, vitrea te Fucinus unda,
te liquidi flevere lacus.

As well, from the Marruvian race, sent by King Archippus, there came
a priest, his helmet decked with leaves of the fruitful olive, most valiant Umbro, who with charm and touch was wont to shed slumber on
the viperous brood and on water snakes of baneful breath, soothing
their wrath and curing their bites by his skill. But he availed not to
heal the stroke of the Dardan spear-point, nor against wounds did
slumberous charms aid him, or herbs culled on Marsian hills. For you
Angitia's grove wept, for you Fucinus' glassy wave, for you the limpid
lakes!... (Fairclough-Goold)

By itself this is one of the most moving descriptions in the poem. The
narrator's apostrophizing of the Marsian place names brings them alive
before us in a stunning example of the pathetic fallacy. We are reminded of Orpheus (in the words of Proteus) lamenting the loss of Eurydice
(*Geo.* 4. 465–66):

te, dulcis coniunx, te solo in litore secum,
te veniente die, te decedente canebat.

He sang to himself of you, sweet wife, on the lonely shore, you as day
comes, you as it departs.

The address has the effect of bringing Eurydice alive before us, and therefore of anticipating proleptically her lover's nearly successful attempt to
restore her from the world of the dead to our terrestrial existence. In the
case of Umbro, beloved by his weeping landscape, there is only death in
the offing. No words or songs have power against the weapons of war,
or at least these weapons. The fury of Aeneas is on a different level of
enmity from vipers and water snakes.[41]

Umbro is in good company. As a *sacerdos* he is linked with Haemonides, priest of Apollo and Diana. He therefore becomes the second priest
that Aeneas kills in his spate of violence. As a magician, he is allied by
Virgil with Magus ("the sorcerer"), Aeneas's first victim to be characterized at length. The description of Umbro in book 7 tells us that his
priestly incantations will have no power against Dardan arms and the
wounds that they inflict. What happens to Magus and to Haemonides

offers further evidence that an enchanter's words or the reverence due religious authority stand no chance against the armament of Aeneas's anger. Virgil need say no more here than that Umbro came from the mountains of the Marsi to remind his readers that already in book 7 the Marsian mage has suffered a parallel fate. The mountains have already done their weeping.[42]

Achilles returns in the next vignette (550–60):

> Tarquitus exsultans contra fulgentibus armis,
> silvicolae Fauno Dryope quem nympha crearat,
> obvius ardenti sese obtulit. ille reducta
> loricam clipeique ingens onus impedit hasta,
> tum caput orantis nequiquam et multa parantis
> dicere deturbat terrae, truncumque tepentem
> provolvens super haec inimico pectore fatur:
> 'istic nunc, metuende, iace. non te optima mater
> condet humi patrioque onerabit membra sepulcro:
> alitibus linquere feris, aut gurgite mersum
> unda feret piscesque impasti vulnera lambent.'

Tarquitus, whom the Nymph Dryope had borne to sylvan Faunus, glorying in his gleaming arms confronted [Aeneas] as he rages. With his spear drawn back [Aeneas] pins the corselet and the shield's huge burden together; then, as [Tarquitus] pleads in vain and prepares to say many things, he knocks his head to the ground, and, rolling forward the warm trunk, he speaks these words from his hostile heart: "Lie there now, you to be feared. No kindliest mother will lay you in the earth or place the burden of your limbs in your ancestral tomb. You will be left for birds of the wild, the wave will bear you along, sunk in its flood, and hungry fish will lick your wounds."

Several motifs from the preceding episodes are taken up again here. Aeneas is afire (*ardenti*, 552) as he at the onset of his rage (*ardens*, 514). He once more looms above his victim (*super*, 556), reflecting his stance before the killing of Haemonides (*superstans*, 540). And yet again he kills a suppliant pleading for mercy (*orantis*, 554), as he had in the case of Magus (*orantis*, 536).[43]

But there is a still richer connection between the Magus and Tarquitus episodes. We observed earlier the allusive links between Virgil's tale of Magus and Homer's description of the story of Lycaon at the opening of *Iliad* 21. In the vignette of the clash between Aeneas and Tarquitus Virgil takes up where he had left Homer in the earlier episode. The killing of Magus is parallel to that of Lycaon (*Iliad* 21. 116–18):

> But Achilles drew his sharp sword and smote him upon the collarbone beside the neck, and all the two-edged sword sank in;...

What follows in Homer, Achilles's curse over the corpse, Virgil now allots to Aeneas (*Iliad* 21. 120–27):

> Achilles then, seizing him by the foot, flung him into the river to be borne away, and exulting over him spoke winged words: "Lie there now among the fish that will lick the blood from your wounds heedlessly, nor will your mother make lament as she lays your corpse on a bier, but whirling Scamander will bear you into the wide bosom of the sea. Many a fish, leaping along the wave, will dart up to the dark ripple to eat the white flesh of Lycaon."

Virgil's changes to his model are many. The eddying stream is replaced by Aeneas himself, who becomes a force of nature as he rolls over the still warm corpse. The prideful scorn of *metuende* ("you to be feared") is missing from Achilles's vaunt. Homer allots no adjective to Lycaon's mother. Her parallel in the *Aeneid* is her designation as *optima* (best of all), and Virgil adds a reference to Tarquitus's father with the mention of *patrio sepulcro*, so that the implicit sorrow of both parents at the death of their son is present before the reader. Lycaon's death takes place within the river itself. Aeneas kills Tarquitus at the edge of the Tiber,[44] on land near water. The topography allows for the horrific development of Achilles's curse. Birds as well as fish, now hungry in Virgil's adaptation, are among the possible devourers of Aeneas's victim.[45]

In all instances Virgil complements and extends Homer, as if, once again, the Roman poet would have us see his hero as a version of Achilles still more vicious than the one presented in *Iliad* 21. But there is a difference crucial to Virgil's presentation. Achilles slays Lycaon by driving the length of his sword into his enemy's body. Aeneas, by contrast, severs the head of his still pleading foe, as if the part of the body that would ordinarily pray is now useless, and then rolls over the corpse. The Greek warrior's method of killing serves as a reminder of the way Aeneas killed Magus and therefore of how Achilles's son Pyrrhus had murdered Priam. But we remember that the death of the Trojan king was as horrible as it was surreal. Pyrrhus buries his sword up to the hilt in his aged victim, but he also decapitates him (*Aen.* 2. 557–58):

> ...iacet ingens litore truncus
> avulsumque umeris caput et sine nomine corpus.

> He lies upon the shore, a huge trunk and head torn from shoulders,
> a body without a name.

Aeneas shortly after glosses one aspect of this scene in words he addresses to his father (2. 662–63):

> iamque aderit multo Priami de sanguine Pyrrhus,
> natum ante ora patris, patrem qui obtruncat ad aras.

> And now Pyrrhus will be here, steeped in Priam's blood, who slaugh-
> ters the son before his father's face, the father at the altars.

Virgil's use of the word *truncus* at 557 urges us to give the verb *obtruncat*
its most literal meaning: to turn the body into a torso by lopping its head
off. Pyrrhus not only kills Priam with his sword thrust full length, he also
decapitates him as well, at his place of refuge.

Virgil therefore helps us make the transition from the Magus episode
to that of Tarquitus in two ways. The first is through Homer. The killing
of Magus borrows from the opening of *Iliad* 21, where Achilles rejects
Lycaon's plea for restraint. Tarquitus's death scene looks to the conclusion of the same story as his conqueror kills and then utters his curse.
In both cases Aeneas reenacts the part of Achilles at his most brutal, and
Virgil seems bent on expanding this malevolence. The second is through
Virgil himself. We have seen how, in his killing of Magus, as he thrusts
his sword up to the hilt into his victim, Aeneas's action parallels him with
Pyrrhus, who slew Priam in the same manner.[46] But, to compound the
horror, Pyrrhus decapitated his suppliant as well.[47] This is also the man-
ner in which Aeneas slays the suppliant Tarquitus.[48]

Thus we also make the transition from the death of Magus to that of
Tarquitus by seeing Aeneas twiceover as Achilles's son Pyrrhus, who sets
the poem's pattern for the heinous murder of suppliants.[49] Just as Virgil's allusiveness divides Homer's story of Lycaon into two parts while
still keeping the parallel between Achilles and Aeneas, so he also sepa-
rates his own startling depiction of the double murder of Priam into two
parts — sword thrust up to the hilt and decapitation. These in turn find
their parallels in the two sections devoted to the deaths of the same two
heroes in *Aeneid* 10. On these occasions through Virgil's artistry Aeneas
is now envisioned for us as Pyrrhus, the still more degenerate son of a

degenerate father, killing one version after another of suppliant Priam in two separate confrontations.[50]

After presenting four more killings in so many lines, Virgil distinguishes the moment with a simile (10. 565–70):

> Aegaeon qualis, centum cui bracchia dicunt
> centenasque manus, quinquaginta oribus ignem
> pectoribusque arsisse, Iovis cum fulmina contra
> tot paribus streperet clipeis, tot stringeret ensis:
> sic toto Aeneas desaevit in aequore victor
> ut semel intepuit mucro.

> Like Aegaeon who men say had a hundred arms and a hundred hands, who blazed with fire from fifty mouths and chests when against the thunderbolts of Jupiter he clanged with as many like shields, he bared as many swords: thus Aeneas in victory vented his rage over the whole plain when once his sword-point grew warm.

When we first meet Aegaeon, "whom the gods call Briareus," in literature, Homer portrays him as a figure of such might that he scares the Olympian gods.[51] The depiction in Hesiod expands the portrayal to include his possession of one hundred arms and fifty heads, and to show him as helper of the Olympians in their battle against the Titans.[52] But Callimachus places him beneath Aetna, presumably as punishment for warring against the gods,[53] and it is of this tradition that Virgil would remind us as Aeneas pursues his violent course.

Virgil emphasizes the enormity of the monster by adding a hundred hands to Hesiod's hundred arms, and the fifty heads gain greater specificity by flashing fire. The first attribute has us ponder the sheer physicality of Aeneas's onslaught. The second makes palpable the fieriness of the hero's inner passion, as *arsisse* draws climactically upon *ardens* (514) and *ardenti* (552).[54] The warmth of Aeneas's sword as it grew hot from blood (*intepuit*) is a reminder of Tarquitus's *truncum tepentem* (555), still warm with blood.

Two lexical novelties further enliven the description. This is the first use of the verb *intepesco* in Latin, and probably only the second appearance of *desaevio*.[55] The first is at *Aeneid* 4. 52, where the rage of a winter storm is the subject. It's presence thus serves here verbally to reinforce the spectacle of Aeneas as a negative force of nature, an emblem of uncontrolled and uncontrollable, passionate wildness, a gigantic body opposing the might, but also the rationality, of Jupiter and his fellow divinities.

We have seen Aegaeon-Briareus once before in the poem, at *Aeneid* 6. 287, where he is one of "many monsters of various beasts" (*multa... variarum monstra ferarum*) that Virgil places before the entrance court leading into the realm of the underworld. Aeneas draws his sword to fight them off, but the Sibyl explains that they are but faint incorporeal forms, with only an outward appearance of shape. Virgil's extraordinary simile in book 10, however, is a reminder that these monsters, like the personified abstractions of mankind's worries and trials that preceded them before the vestibule of Dis, not only inhabit human bodies but cause those bodies to become incorporations of their characteristics. The simile as a rhetorical device complements its contents. It serves as the semblance of a representation. Aeneas is only a likeness of Aegaeon, but nevertheless an important likeness, both materially, as the savage embodiment of seemingly limitless physical bestiality at work, and, spiritually and morally, as the personification of inclemency spurred by the need for vengeance carried to an irrational extreme.

A single victim is the center of the next episode (10. 570–74):

> ...quin ecce Niphaei
> quadriiugis in equos adversaque pectora tendit.
> atque illi longe gradientem et dira frementem
> ut videre, metu versi retroque ruentes
> effunduntque ducem rapiuntque ad litora currus.

> Now see: he proceeds toward the four-yoked horses of Niphaeus and their facing chests. When they saw him striding lengthily and roaring dreadfully, they turned about in terror and rushing backward they throw their master and drag the chariot to the shore.

As ServiusD notes,[56] there is no mention of Niphaeus's killing or of whether the animals dragged his body, like that of Troilus,[57] as well as their chariot to the river's edge. Rather, the poet has us watch (*ecce*) as the horses watch (*videre*), and what we see, picking up a hint from the Aegaeon simile, is the powerful effect Aeneas exerts, emanating not from what he does but simply from his physical presence alone.

Virgil qualifies this phenomenon with two participles and their modifiers, placed centrally in the description. The first is *longe gradientem*. Servius's gloss is to the point: *longis gradibus incedentem: et est militaris incessus* ("striding with long steps; the stride is a soldier's").[58] But etymology helps us see that Aeneas represents not any soldier but one of special exemplarity: Mars. The god of war, we recall, was apostrophized at line 542 as *rex Gradive*. The epithet is most expressively explained by Paulus Festus: *Gradivus Mars appellatus est a gradiendo in bella ultro citroque...* ("Mars is called Gradivus from striding [*gradiendo*] to and fro into battle").[59] Thus it is Aeneas as a gigantic epiphany of the war god whose approach frightens the four horses of Niphaeus.

Virgil calls on a further sense, hearing, with the second participle, *dira frementem*. The animals only need to see and hear Aeneas. But this is also the only use of the phrase in extant Latin literature, and it has a particular point.[60] The Aeneas who attacks Caeculus and Umbro with fury (*furit*, 545) and who for the final word of his frenzied behavior here is called *furens* (604), during his extended bout of rage takes the form of an avenging Fury[61] just as he is also a type of omnipotent Mars. To roar dreadfully is to give voice to the desperate need for retaliation that motivates the plethora of killings that Virgil has put before us in his own bravura variations.

The final episode in the series is both the longest and the most dramatic (575–601):

> Interea biiugis infert se Lucagus albis
> in medios fraterque Liger: sed frater habenis
> flectit equos, strictum rotat acer Lucagus ensem.
> haud tulit Aeneas tanto fervore furentis;
> inruit adversaque ingens apparuit hasta.
> cui Liger: 'non Diomedis equos nec currum cernis Achilli
> aut Phrygiae campos: nunc belli finis et aevi
> his dabitur terris.' vesano talia late
> dicta volant Ligeri. sed non et Troius heros
> dicta parat contra, iaculum nam torquet in hostis.
> Lucagus ut pronus pendens in verbera telo
> admonuit biiugos, proiecto dum pede laevo
> aptat se pugnae, subit oras hasta per imas
> fulgentis clipei, tum laevum perforat inguen;
> excussus curru moribundus volvitur arvis.
> quem pius Aeneas dictis adfatur amaris:
> 'Lucage, nulla tuos currus fuga segnis equorum
> prodidit aut vanae vertere ex hostibus umbrae:
> ipse rotis saliens iuga deseris.' haec ita fatus
> arripuit biiugos; frater tendebat inertis
> infelix palmas curru delapsus eodem:
> 'per te, per qui te talem genuere parentes,
> vir Troiane, sine hanc animam et miserere precantis.'

pluribus oranti Aeneas: 'haud talia dudum
dicta dabas. morere et fratrem ne desere frater.'
tum latebras animae pectus mucrone recludit.

Meanwhile Lucagus and Liger his brother charge into the midst with their two white steeds; the brother guides the horses with the reins, fierce Lucagus brandishes his drawn sword. Aeneas did not withstand their raging with such vehemence. He rushed in and loomed huge with his menacing spear. To him Liger..."You are not now looking at the horses of Diomedes or the chariot of Achilles or the plains of Phrygia. Now an end to your warring and to your life will be given you in this land." Such words fly abroad from Liger in his madness. But the Trojan hero doesn't prepare words in reply, for he whirls his javelin against his enemies. As Lucagus, leaning forward to the stroke, urged on his pair with his sword, while with his left foot in front he prepared for the fight, the spear passes through the innermost layers of the gleaming shield, then pierces the left groin. Thrown from his chariot he rolls on the ground, dying. Pious Aeneas addresses him with bitter words: "Lucagus, no cowardly flight on the part of your horses betrayed your chariot nor did the enemy's empty shadows make them turn. You yourself, leaping from the wheels, abandon your team." After these words he seized the two horses. His unfortunate brother, also slipping down from the chariot, outstretched his powerless hands: "By yourself, Trojan hero, by the parents who bore such a one, spare this life and have pity on my prayer." While he pleads still more, Aeneas: "Such were not the words you just uttered. Die and do not as a brother abandon your brother." Then with his sword point he lays open his chest, life's hiding place.

The passage is a carefully constructed dialogue between words and deeds. The words consist of a boastful utterance and then a prayer for mercy on the part of Liger, alternating with two speeches by Aeneas, the first directed to Lucagus, the second to his brother. The striking anaphora of *dicta* and *non dicta* at 584–85 brings the distinction to the fore: words, whether challenging or pleading, have no effect against the looming presence of Aeneas and his spear.

The episode is also structured so as to emphasize the word *frater* and thus the relationship of brother to brother. The initial lines offer an example of chiasmus — Lucagus, *frater*, Liger, *frater*, Lucagus — that both calls attention to the two individual names through framing and centrality and emphasizes the notion of fraternity that goes with them.[62] There is also a careful balance to the whole, with a double use of *frater* in its second line —

in medios fraterque Liger; sed frater habenis —

and in its penultimate

dicta dabas. morere et fratrem ne desere frater...

This parallel doubleness is echoed, and reinforced, by the fact that the brothers drive a two-horse chariot. In fact, three out of Virgil's eight uses of *biiugis* or *biiugus* are contained in these lines.

Near the center of the episode comes one of Virgil's most striking applications of the adjective *pius* to Aeneas. He is pious, no doubt, because he remembers his loyalty to Pallas and Evander, as the opening of his *aristeia* taught us. But here, at its climax and conclusion, we watch as the presumed epitome of the loyalty son brings to father kills first one brother and then the second.

The final lines are a climax in another sense, pulling together motifs from the whole passage. The beginning of Liger's appeal for mercy (*per te, per qui te talem genuere parentes*) is a reminder of the opening of Magus's plea for restraint (*per patrios manis et spes surgentis Iuli / te precor*, 524–25) whose mention of his own life (*animam*) anticipates the double use of the same word at 598, in Liger's prayer, and at 601, in the narrative. Likewise, the participle *oranti* (599) serves to reflect the use of the same verb at 536 (of Magus) and at 554 (of Tarquitus). Virgil thus asks us, as *pius* Aeneas kills Liger, to remember that he has also previously killed two other warriors asking for mercy on his part. So at the place of climax, Virgil's hero not only obliterates two symbols of family unity — brother at work with brother — he also fails to acknowledge an appeal to Venus and Anchises, the goddess of love and the father who in the underworld had directed him to spare an enemy once he has been brought low. The two pieties face each other, in the reader's mind at least, as Aeneas acts, and Virgil offers us sufficient evidence, here and elsewhere, to guide our opinion about the choice that the hero makes.

Virgil's brief description of the second killing also brings a forceful reminder of the past (601): *Tum latebras animae pectus mucrone recludit.* The only other occasion where the poet uses *pectus* with a form of *recludo* is at 4. 63–64, where Dido consults entrails as part of her attempt to appease the gods and to determine the future:

> ...pecudumque reclusis
> pectoribus inhians spirantia consulit exta.

...agape at the opened breasts of the animals, she consults their breathing entrails.

Aeneas in book 10 has no need to practice extispicy. Virgil, however, by his reminder of Dido's recourse to animal sacrifice, has us see the death of Liger as, metaphorically, a final human offering in the string of victims Aeneas sacrifices here as implicit offerings to Pallas.[63] He thus not only brings unity to the lines he devoted to the hero's rampage, but also prepares us for the final sacrifice with which the epic concludes as Aeneas's rage works its horror for one last time.

The Liger-Lucagus episode also reminds us of Achilles again, this time both directly and indirectly. Liger's arrogant words to Aeneas refer us to the two occasions in the *Iliad* where the hero of Virgil's epic is saved from death at the hands of a victorious opponent. The first takes place in book 5, where Aphrodite and Apollo rescue him from Diomedes, the second occurs in book 20, where Poseidon protects him from Achilles. But what Liger doesn't realize is that he is in fact challenging not Aeneas alone so much as Aeneas as Virgil's version of Achilles redivivus, and that this time there will be no saving divinity to intervene. Allusion again supports Virgil's equation, for the phrase *Phrygiae campos* (582) draws the reader's attention back to Catullus 64, a poem that we have already seen to be on Virgil's mind at the beginning of the passage. We find ourselves a few lines before the comparison of Achilles to a reaper, as the Fates take us to Troy and the hero's prowess (64. 343–44):

> non illi quisquam bello se conferet heros,
> cum Phrygii Teucro manabunt sanguine <campi,>...[64]

...nor will any hero confront him in battle when the Phrygian fields will run with Trojan blood...

Virgil in fact places us in a position to observe a new version of the fighting on the "Phrygian fields" with the roles reversed, as Trojan Aeneas again takes the place of Achilles, drenching the fields with blood.[65]

Three further lines serve as summary (10. 602–4):

talia per campos edebat funera ductor
Dardanius torrentis aquae vel turbinis atri
more furens.

Such were the deaths the Trojan leader caused throughout the fields,
as he rages like rushing water or a black whirlwind.[66]

In book 2 Aeneas, as he gives ear to the sounds of Troy's destruction,
compares himself to an unaware shepherd listening to the roar of fire
supported "by raging South Winds" (*furentibus Austris*, 2. 304) or of a
devastating mountain torrent (*torrens*, 305). By book 10 he has become
no longer the passive sufferer of ruin but the ravaging force of nature
itself.

If Aeneas as *torrens* looks backward into the epic, *turbinis atri* anticipates its conclusion. We will soon be watching Aeneas's spear as its blow
brings Turnus to his knees (12. 923–25):

> ...volat atri turbinis instar
> exitium dirum hasta ferens orasque recludit
> loricae...

The spear flies like a black whirlwind, bringing dread destruction,
and lays open the rims of his corselet...

In book 10 the dark tornado summarizes Aeneas's general fury on the
battlefield. In the epic's final moments it represents the hero's particular wrath, as it "uncloses" the edges of Turnus's cuirass just as Aeneas's
sword "uncloses" the breast of Tarquitus to let his life go free.[67] Tarquitus
pleads as does Turnus,[68] and both ask for pity, the one for himself, the
other for his father.[69]

Much intervenes in the poem between the two episodes, including a
moment when an unarmed *pius* Aeneas pleads for an end to anger between the fighters.[70] But, as one black whirlwind leads to another, so the
reader connects the spate of slaughter in book 10 with the final killing in
book 12. There Turnus also pleads for mercy, and Aeneas is reminded of
his father and hesitates, but Pallas — and the piety of revenge — at the
last gain control, and Aeneas, "set aflame by the Furies" (*furiis accensus*),
buries his sword in his opponent's chest. As in book 10, fury remains
ascendant in the hero's mind as his angry deed brings conclusion to the
epic.

We end the poem as the *Iliad* begins, with the anger of Achilles. But the conclusion of book 10 only brings a pause in the spate of Aeneas's killings. Nevertheless, the book's final two victims of his sword-blade deserve special mention by us just as they receive place of honor in Virgil's text, namely Lausus and Mezentius. The plot can be quickly summarized. The Etruscan king Mezentius's abominable conduct toward his people is such that, according to an ancient soothsayer, it aroused their "righteous resentment" (*iustus dolor*, *Aen.* 8. 500–1) and "deserved wrath" (*merita ira*, 501), and he has been forced into exile.[71] Virgil's poetic practice emphasizes the probity of this response. The only occasions in the poem where the nouns *dolor* and *ira* are given positive accolades are here, and, for *ira* alone, book 10, line 714, all in connection with Mezentius. As the *haruspex* would have it, the Etruscan race had every right to respond as it did to their cruel ruler.

But Virgil brilliantly complicates his already original treatment of the Mezentius legend by having the king followed into exile by his devoted son Lausus. The latter's allegiance doesn't stop there. In the book's final scene of battle, Aeneas first wounds the father who is eased off the field of combat under the protection of his son. He then kills Lausus, who, as the narrator puts it, foolishly continues to rouse his wrath after he utters the words (*Aen.* 10. 811–12):

> 'quo moriture ruis maioraque viribus audes?
> fallit te incautum pietas tua.'

"Where do you rush, about to die, and dare deeds greater than your strength? Your piety betrays you in your imprudence."

He then kills the wounded father who has returned vainly to battle to revenge his son, abstract piety taking concrete form.

We end the book dwelling not so much on Aeneas's anger as on our pious hero's killing the incorporation of piety. Virgil memorializes the moment with some of his most impressive lines as the victor gazes at the corpse of the youth he has just slain (821–24):

> At vero ut vultum vidit morientis et ora,
> ora modis Anchisiades pallentia miris,
> ingemuit miserans graviter dextramque tetendit,
> et mentem patriae subiit pietatis imago.

But when the son of Anchises saw the face and features of him as he dies, the features pale in marvelous ways, he groaned deeply in pity and stretched out his right hand, and the reflection of paternal piety entered his mind.

The passage is extraordinary in several ways.[72] This is the last time in the poem where Aeneas is called Anchisiades, as if Virgil, for a special reason, was intent on reminding us of Aeneas's own filial responsibilities toward his father at the very moment when he kills first a son shielding his father and then the father himself. But it is the phrase *patriae pietatis imago* that is most striking, not least for its ambiguity. Critics are divided about its meaning: Does it refer to Aeneas's *pietas* toward his own father or to that of Lausus toward Mezentius?[73] Since we are dealing with a poet of Virgil's genius, the answer is that both nuances must be available to the reader. Only after he has slain the son does Aeneas come to realize the emblematic quality of the person he has killed. It is with some irony that he calls himself *pius* two lines later (826). He has just slain someone who, in death, reminds him, as Virgil reminds us, both of Lausus's loyalty to Mezentius and of his own devotion to Anchises — an aspect of the scene that has already been suggested by the preceding use of the patronymic Anchisiades at the moment of Aeneas's realization.

Lausus and Mezentius are not portrayed by Virgil as suppliants, once proud, now praying for restraint, as is Turnus at the epic's end, and so Anchises's dictum about victors sparing their abased foes is not strictly operative as a gauge by which to judge Aeneas's conduct here. Nevertheless, there is something more than a little disquieting about the way Virgil chooses to end the book in which Aeneas's violence is most patent. The *pietas* for which he is notorious is now corrupted by the hero himself. His presumed devotion to Anchises and to the moderation his father preaches is virtually abandoned by Aeneas as he does to death someone who richly incorporates the piety he first neglects, and then understands, but after it is too late to stay his hand.

As we have said, the spate of slaughter into which Aeneas launches after the death of Pallas leads in due course to the death of Turnus at the epic's end. The provocative deaths of Lausus and Mezentius serve partially as a transition in Aeneas's fatal progress. We will look at the finale in detail later. But before that we have to turn back to the opening books and to the initiation of the parallels between Aeneas and Achilles, the "overturner of the realm of Priam" (*Priami regnorum eversor*) as he is called in book 12,[74] and between Aeneas and Achilles's son, Pyrrhus.[75] In the first four books Aeneas is only a symbolic destroyer of cities. By the time that we reach the epic's conclusion, he is literally in the process of demolishing Latinus's city not long before he kills his last suppliant. But we have almost already arrived, at least spiritually, at such a moment in book 4 when Dido can turn to her sister Anna, as her surrogate, and say (4. 424):

> 'I, soror, atque hostem supplex adfare superbum...'

> "Go, sister, and as a suppliant address our proud foe..."

It is Aeneas the prideful, at least in Anna's view, who must be supplicated. And who will restrain him?

In the next two chapters I will turn to an investigation into Aeneas, ancestor of Rome and Romans to come, in his role as figurative and then literal destroyer of cities.

CHAPTER 3

Aeneas Eversor Troiae

HAMLET: "...Roasted in wrath and fire
And thus o'ersized with coagulate gore,
With eyes like carbuncles, the hellish Pyrrhus
Old grandsire Priam seeks."
    Shakespeare, *Hamlet*, Act II, Scene 2

I N HIS DETAILING of the frenzy of revenge on which Aeneas embarks
in book 10 after Turnus's slaying of Pallas, we have seen how Virgil
draws analogies between Aeneas and both Achilles and his son, Pyrrhus.
We have grown to expect the first analogy already in book 8 where the
ekphrasis of the shield, made by Vulcan at the request of Venus, draws
the reader's attention back to the description of Hephaistos's shield in
Iliad 18. Virgil keeps the connection alive at an earlier moment in book
10, where Aeneas is first sighted by the Rutulians as he journeys down
the river (270–75):

> ardet apex capiti tristisque a vertice flamma
> funditur et vastos umbo vomit aureus ignis:
> non secus ac liquida si quando nocte cometae
> sanguinei lugubre rubent, aut Sirius ardor
> ille sitim morbosque ferens mortalibus aegris
> nascitur et laevo contristat lumine caelum.

On the hero's head the helmet peak blazes, and a dreadful flame
streams from its top, and the shield's golden boss spouts floods of fire
— just as when in the clear night comets glow blood-red and baneful;
or as fiery Sirius, that bearer of drought and pestilence to feeble mortals, rises and saddens the sky with baleful light. (Fairclough-Goold)

The first two lines look to *Iliad* 18. 205–6, but there the gleam that arises
from Achilles's head is further developed and compared to fires emanating from a city under siege (207–10). This latent parallel would seem an
inauspicious one for the ancestral founder of Rome who will soon initiate
the razing of Latinus's city. The similes that follow find their Homeric
source at *Iliad* 22. 26–31, where Achilles is about to begin the fatal pursuit
of Hector, who awaits him before the gates of Troy.[76] In the next chapter we will trace the further evolution of Aeneas's role as city destroyer
and as killer of a new Hector, likewise wearing the armor of someone to
whom he is close. But before we examine in detail the epic's final book
we must return to its start to watch the initiation of these and other

themes that we mentioned earlier. It is in the opening quartet of books that Virgil first casts Aeneas as a character who shares elements with those of Achilles or Pyrrhus, establishing him as a city destroyer, though still metaphoric, and first displaying the particular savagery that results from his anger.

Let us turn at the start to the poem's initial ekphrasis, the depiction, in the epic's first book, of episodes taking place in the time leading up to Troy's fall that Dido has had fashioned as murals for her temple to Juno. With Aeneas we watch the portrayal of Greeks and Trojans in pursuit of each other, we view Diomedes and the horses of Rhesus, the death of Troilus, Trojan women in prayer to Athena, the ransom of Hector, Aeneas among the Greek leaders, Memnon next to last, and at the end Penthesilea. We are essentially surveying, and contemplating along with the Trojan visitor, steps in the story of Troy's demise. The episodes of Rhesus and Troilus are totemic: Diomedes prevents the horses from cropping the grass of Troy (otherwise, according to an oracle, the city could not be taken), Troilus is killed (otherwise, legend had it, the city would remain invulnerable). Athena is implacable. Hector, pivotal hero of Troy, is killed, as are allies who have come from the outside, Memnon and, last of all, Penthesilea.[77]

There are motifs that thread through the description. The old king, Priam, is mentioned on three occasions, both apart from and within the ekphrasis proper. But it is the presence of Achilles that dominates the whole climactically. He is named four times, in each instance at the end of an hexameter. The initial summary of what Aeneas sees ends with (458)

> Atridas Priamumque et saevum ambobus Achillem.

> the sons of Atreus and Priam and Achilles savage to both.

The Greek hero's ferocity affects each side in the conflict. And the first scene ends with similar force, as we focus on the helmeted warrior (467–68):

> hac fugerent Grai, premeret Troiana iuventus;
> hac Phryges, instaret curru cristatus Achilles.

[Aeneas saw] here the Greeks in flight, the Trojan youth in pursuit; here the Trojans [in flight], crested Achilles in his chariot pressing forward.

It is Achilles who kills Troilus, Hector, Memnon, and Penthesilea.

There is a distinct erotic theme here, also. According to inherited legend, Achilles was the lover of Troilus and Penthesilea, and the *Iliad* itself highlights the story of the Greek hero killing the killer of his companion Patroclus.

We will return to this topic when studying the poem's conclusion. Here it is important not to finesse one of the most masterly details in Virgil's presentation. For the final vignette, showing Penthesilea leading her forces, Virgil drops all ekphrastic signposts.[78] We are told of no one watching; no deictic pointers place us, temporally or spatially, in relationship to other episodes. Penthesilea is not yet in fact the victim of Achilles but very much alive (490–93):

> ducit Amazonidum lunatis agmina peltis
> Penthesilea furens mediisque in milibus ardet,
> aurea subnectens exsertae cingula mammae
> bellatrix, audetque viris concurrere virgo.

Frenzied Penthesilea leads her squadrons of Amazons with their crescent-shaped shields, and rages in the midst of her thousands, a female warrior, buckling her golden girdle beneath her naked breast: a virgin she dares join in conflict with men.

The transition from ekphrasis to narrative is doubly masterful on Virgil's part. We move smoothly from Penthesilea, leading her troops toward battle in what, for all appearances, could be the poem's narrative present, to Dido in the actual story line, making her royal progress toward the temple itself.[79] This brilliant evolution, however, has its ominous irony. A surrogate Achilles is also equally present, poised to become Dido's lover and, vicariously, her killer as well as, metaphorically, the destroyer of her city when old Troy is replaced by new Carthage.[80] Let us watch some of the highlights of this development.

The next stage in the figurative destruction of Dido falls to Venus and her son Cupid who, according to the goddess's thoughts (659–60):

> ...donis...furentem
> incendat reginam atque ossibus implicet ignem.

by his gifts might set aflame the maddened queen and enfold fire in her bones.

The gifts from Aeneas, with their rich symbolism, are a veil worn by Helen as she embarked for her illicit marriage, and a scepter borne by Ilione, Priam's eldest daughter, who was to commit suicide. As in the hero's incipient description of Troy's literal downfall, *dona* combine with *doli* to promote Dido's symbolic ruin in Venus's further plotting, as she announces to her son (673–74):

> 'quocirca capere ante dolis et cingere flamma
> reginam meditor.'[81]

"Wherefore I plan beforehand to seize the queen by deceits and to gird her with flames."

The image of destructive fire is woven through the subsequent lines (688, 713) and is revived immediately at the start of the fourth book (2, 23). To that of flames Virgil's narrator soon adds the metaphor of siege (717–19):

> ...haec oculis, haec pectore toto
> haeret et interdum gremio fovet inscia Dido
> insidat quantus miserae deus.

She clings with her eyes, she clings with her whole heart, and repeatedly lovesick Dido fondles him in her lap, ignorant of how mighty a god possesses her.

The god who settles in her lap is also lying in wait for the moment of capture. Once again, as we prepare to hear Aeneas's tale of the *insidiae* that brought doom to Troy,[82] we are witnessing a figurative parallel occurring in the life of Dido. Then, as the book concludes, just before the start of the hero's story, we learn about the smitten queen's requests for information (750–52):

> multa super Priamo rogitans, super Hectore multa;
> nunc quibus Aurorae venisset filius armis,
> nunc quales Diomedis equi, nunc quantus Achilles.

...asking much about Priam, much about Hector; now of the armor in which the son of Aurora came; now of what sort the horses of Diomedes, now of the grandeur of Achilles.

We know that Dido already apprehends a great deal about her chosen subjects. She has, after all, monumentalized them on the temple's walls. Iteration, we presume and as book 4 confirms,[83] will only fan love's flames. But the narrator has a specific point to make. We have seen how the presence of Achilles dominated the earlier ekphrasis and how the prominence given his name rhetorically complemented the description's scope. But the Greek hero, as we also saw, is already at hand in the figure of Aeneas, whom Virgil now carefully allies with Venus and Cupid.[84]

We learn little further about Achilles in the hero's forthcoming narrative because he is dead by the time the narrative begins. But in fact the conclusion of the ekphrasis has taught us that he is still very much alive, symbolically, in the person of Aeneas, initiating the process of destroying his new lover. At 12. 545, as we saw, the narrator calls Achilles "the destroyer of the realms of Priam" (*Priami regnorum eversor*). We will soon bear witness to Aeneas's tale of Priam's death and Troy's doom. But the same Aeneas-Achilles is also embarked metaphorically on the destruction of another ruler and another city. To watch this new history we must turn ahead to book 4.

Already on fire, according to the vivid images of the book's opening lines, Dido herself describes the collapse of her resolve in the face of love shortly thereafter (22–23):

> 'solus hic inflexit sensus animumque labantem
> impulit.'

"He alone has bent my feelings and overthrown my collapsing resolve."

Virgil draws the metaphor from 2. 463–65, where Aeneas tells of the Trojans tearing off a turret from Priam's palace to hurl at the approaching Greeks below:

> [turrim] adgressi ferro circum, qua summa labantis
> iuncturas tabulata dabant, convellimus altis
> sedibus impulimusque.

> Assailing [the tower] round about with iron, where the stories at the top presented collapsing joints, we wrenched it from its lofty position and threw it over.

The crumpling of Dido's steadfast loyalty to her dead husband is compared to a moment in the demise of Troy where Aeneas and his followers rend apart one of Troy's battlements. The Trojan warrior, a participant in Troy's literal demise, becomes already at the book's start the metaphoric destroyer of Dido's house and kingdom.

Dido herself picks up the figurative chain at 318, during her first address to Aeneas, when speaking of her "tottering house" (*domus labantis*), where *domus* stands both for her household and dynasty as well as for the city that is a crucial component of each. She confirms the formulation in her concluding words where, she remarks, if she only had a baby Aeneas for company (330):

> 'non equidem omnino capta ac deserta viderer.'

> "I wouldn't seem so completely captured and desolate."

Already in her mind she is like a city, thoroughly vanquished and then left abandoned.[85] The narrator elaborates the horror of her self-portrait at 465–68, where we are told of Dido's nightmare vision:

> ...agit ipse furentem
> in somnis ferus Aeneas, semperque relinqui
> sola sibi, semper longam incomitata videtur
> ire viam et Tyrios deserta quaerere terra,...

> In her dreams savage Aeneas himself drives her, frenzied, and ever she seems to herself to be left alone, ever to embark without companions on a lengthy journey, and to seek the Tyrians in a desolate land.[86]

Earlier in the book, Aeneas had been compared to a shepherd "ruthlessly hurling his shafts" (*agens telis*, 71) at a deer that he has, in his ignorance, already wounded.[87] In her dream Aeneas is now no longer a *pastor nescius* but simply *ferus* (wild), a human beast driving another human.

In between Dido's speeches and the heightening of her madness that leads to suicide, Virgil offers one of his many extraordinary similes that help us deepen our response to the story line. Aeneas, now pious (*pius*, 393), presumably because he is obedient to the will of fate, and like Dido was earlier, "tottering in his mind from love" (*animum labefactus amore*, 395), starts earnest preparations for departure. To draw the reader into sharing the emotionality of the moment, Virgil resorts to the second person for one of the poem's few occasions in the midst of epic's third-person presentation (401):

> migrantis cernas totaque ex urbe ruentis....

You might see [the Trojans] on the move and rushing from the whole city....

But there is another "you" involved with this vision — Dido herself (408–11):

> quis tibi tum, Dido, cernenti talia sensus,
> quosve dabas gemitus, cum litora fervere late
> prospiceres arce ex summa, totumque videres
> misceri ante oculos tantis clamoribus aequor!

What feelings then were yours, Dido, viewing such a sight, what groans did you utter when from the top of the citadel you beheld the shore astir far and wide and you saw before your eyes the whole sea bustling with bold shouts.

Apostrophe, especially as utilized in such a passionately charged example, is as rare in epic narrative as second-person address. The effect here is intimately to connect you, Virgil's hearer and reader, with you, Dido, the book's chief protagonist. Aeneas may be fated to depart for Italy, but it is with the Carthaginian queen that we bear witness and in whose suffering we share.

Between the two descriptions comes the enriching simile (402–7):

> ac velut ingentem formicae farris acervum
> cum populant hiemis memores tectoque reponunt,
> it nigrum campis agmen praedamque per herbas
> convectant calle angusto; pars grandia trudunt
> obnixae frumenta umeris, pars agmina cogunt
> castigantque moras, opere omnis semita fervet.

Even as, when ants, mindful of winter, lay waste a huge heap of grain and store it in their home, a black column makes its way over the fields and on a narrow track they bring together their booty through the grass; some, straining with their shoulders, shove the huge grains, some marshal the ranks and chastise delay; the whole path is astir with the work.

Apollonius has a brief simile on swarms of earth-burrowing ants, the only one in ancient literature, that Virgil may have had in mind.[88] But, as usual, Virgil is himself his best critic. Commentators rightly point for a parallel to the *Aeneid*'s three bee similes, in particular 1. 430–36:

> qualis apes aestate nova per florea rura
> exercet sub sole labor, cum gentis adultos
> educunt fetus, aut cum liquentia mella
> stipant et dulci distendunt nectare cellas,
> aut onera accipiunt venientum, aut agmine facto
> ignavum fucos pecus a praesepibus arcent;
> fervet opus redolentque thymo fraglantia mella.

Even as in the newness of summer bees go about their task in the sunshine through the flowery fields, when they lead forth the grown young of their race, or when they pack in liquid honey and stretch their cells with sweet nectar, or receive the loads from incomers or, with battle line drawn up, prevent the lazy herd of drones from their folds; their work is aglow, and the fragrant honey is redolent of thyme.

The various verbal repetitions, especially the echo of *fervet opus* in *opere fervet* in the final lines of each, mean that Virgil would have us see the two similes as mirror images of each other. The complementary inversions are telling, therefore. In moving from summer to winter, from sunshine to a black column, we turn from the resourceful to the parasitic, from creation to depredation, from constructive to destructive discipline. The Carthaginian artisanship, for which the apian world offers analogy, well exemplifies a world of political and ethical order, of aesthetic quality, of cultural accomplishment. Trojan activity, though it exemplifies the virtues of prudence and frugality, works in a largely opposite way from that of the bees. Opportunism is on display.

Virgil allows himself a pointed irony in one further echo between books 1 and 4. When Ilioneus addresses Dido on behalf of the Trojans before Aeneas has made his appearance, he assures her (527–28):

> 'non nos aut ferro Libycos populare penatis
> venimus, aut raptas ad litora vertere praedas.'

"We have not come either to despoil Libyan homes with the sword, or to drive shoreward booty that we have plundered."

Yet the repetitions of *populare* and *praeda*, from speech in book 1 to simile in book 4, illustrate that this is exactly what the Trojans have figuratively done. They have come as a symbolic army on the march and despoiled a city. Virgil will further expand his metaphorical pattern as the book draws to a close. Let us look for a moment at other details in the simile with the help of Virgil himself.

The phrase *it nigrum campis agmen* has a particularly ominous quality about it. The word *agmen* anticipates its plurality in *agmina* (406) as the simile grows in intensity. But the whole phrase looks ahead to the moment in book 12 when Aeneas returns to battle after his wounding (450):

> ille volat campoque atrum rapit agmen aperto.

He speeds and on the open plain sweeps his black column along.[89]

Already in book 4 Aeneas is metaphorically in charge of a marauding army of which Dido and her city are the psychological and literal victims.

Much the same resonance can be sensed from the verb *convectant* (405). Virgil's only other use of the word occurs at 7. 749, where, as part of the catalogue of Latin warriors, we are introduced to the Aequi, who go about life wearing armor and who live off of booty that they have seized from others (748–49):

> armati terram exercent semperque recentis
> convectare iuvat praedas et vivere rapto.

They work the earth while in armor, and it ever gives them pleasure to bring together their fresh booty and to sustain life through what they seized.

Once again we find a parallel in the militaristic realities of Italian tribal life with the symbolic plundering of Carthage and its ruler by Aeneas and his fellow Trojans.

Let us now turn to the end of the book and to the reaction of her people to the death of Dido (665–71):

> ...it clamor ad alta
> atria; concussam bacchatur Fama per urbem.
> lamentis gemituque et femineo ululatu
> tecta fremunt, resonat magnis plangoribus aether,
> non aliter quam si immissis ruat hostibus omnis

> Karthago aut antiqua Tyros, flammasque furentes
> culmina perque hominum volvantur perque deorum.

Cries rise toward the heights of the palace. Rumor rushes wildly through the stricken city. The houses resound with lamentations, and moaning, and the keening of women. The heavens resound with great wailing. It is as if all of Carthage or ancient Tyre were collapsing from an enemy's inrush, and raging flames were swirling through the roofs of humans, through the roofs of gods.

We have seen the developing portrait of Dido as a city first under siege, then left captive and abandoned. Virgil now portrays Dido and her city as a symbiotic entity. The suicide of Dido anticipates, or better, is the symbolic complement to the ruin of Carthage. As so often in ancient literature, ruler and ruled are interdependent. Here the death of one parallels the death of the other. As her sister Anna puts it (4. 682–83):

> 'extinxti te meque, soror, populumque patresque
> Sidonios urbemque tuam.'

"You have destroyed yourself and me, sister, and the people, and the Sidonian fathers and your city."

Allusion here works in two directions. Virgil would have us first think of a parallel simile in a setting that bears comparison with the conclusion of the fourth book of the *Aeneid*, namely Homer's description of the death of Hector. Let me pick up as we watch the reaction of his parents to the mutilation of the Trojan hero's corpse (*Iliad* 22. 405–13):

> So was [Hector's] head all befouled with dust; but his mother tore her hair and flung far her gleaming veil and uttered a cry exceeding loud at the sight of her son. And a piteous groan did his father utter, and around them the people were given over to wailing and groaning throughout the city. To this was it most like, as though all beetling Ilios were utterly burning with fire. And the people were barely able to hold back the old man in his frenzy, eager as he was to go out from the Dardanian gates.

The sorrow of Hecuba and Priam is replaced in Virgil's scenario by the lament of Dido's sister, Anna, but in each case a simile draws attention to how crucial is one particular individual for a city's survival or demise.

But the particularities of the simile are important here. Hector's death betokens the fiery collapse of Troy just as the fiery demise of Carthage eventuates from the suicide of Dido on her funeral pyre.

Virgil has prepared us also for another similarity. We have earlier seen Aeneas enter Dido's life as a type of Achilles confronting Penthesilea as both lover and, in due course, killer. The ekphrasis that tells of final events in the history of Troy leads out into Virgil's text in two ways. It anticipates the conclusion of Troy's tale in Aeneas's powerful narrative to Dido that constitutes the epic's second book. But as the queen listens, she is also catching fire, a fire that gradually leads, literally, to her fiery demise, metaphorically, to the doom of her city in flames. The Trojans may be a marauding army of ants, but their leader is an Achilles, dooming at once lover and city, destructive Greek masquerading, by means of Virgil's genius, as Trojan.

And Virgil is careful to remind us, also through allusion, of the ruin of Troy.[90] The vocabulary of the simile itself looks back to book 2. The collapse of Carthage (*ruat*, 669) is a reminder of the ruin of Troy (*ruit a culmine Troia*, 2. 290).[91] *Immissis hostibus* (669) recalls Aeneas's telling of the Greeks rushing into Priam's palace (*immissi Danai*, 2. 495). And the phrase *flammaeque furentes / culmina per...volvantur* (670–71) echoes *flammas ad culmina iactant* (2. 478). But lines 665–68 offer a particular reminder of 2. 486–88:

> at domus interior gemitu miseroque tumultu
> miscetur, penitusque cavae plangoribus aedes
> femineis ululant; ferit aurea sidera clamor.

> But the inner part of the house was a confusion of moaning and pitiable uproar, and the chambered dwelling keened with the wailing of women. The cries strike the golden stars.

The similarities between the two descriptions are often remarked upon, but it is essential to remember what is actually happening at this moment in the narrative of Troy's downfall when reminded of it at the death of Dido.[92] The Greeks are in the process of breaking into the palace of Priam, and at their head is Pyrrhus, son of Achilles (2. 491):

> instat vi patria Pyrrhus...

> Pyrrhus presses forward, with the force of his father...

And the particular goal of his onslaught is first Priam's son Polites, then the old king himself. Polites dies, "pouring out his life with much blood" (2. 532), before the faces of his parents. Then grasping the hair of the father, as he slips in the blood of his son, Pyrrhus buries his sword up to the hilt in the side of Troy's ancient ruler.

We have noted how Aeneas performs the same gesture when, in book 10, he kills the suppliant Magus. We now find ourselves watching the model for Aeneas's later behavior. But the path that brought us back to book 2, and to the chronological start of the *Aeneid*'s narrative, was the parallel between the lamentation of women in book 4, at the death of Dido, and in book 2, as we prepare for the death of Priam, and for Troy's final hours. The last was brought about by Pyrrhus, but with copious reminders of his father Achilles by Aeneas-Virgil in the telling. The first was literally the result of self-slaughter. But, as we have seen, Aeneas and Achilles, by analogy, are ever in the background. Pyrrhus kills the aged king whose death means the demise of his city. And by reminding us of the death of Hector and the collapse of Troy at the moment of Dido's death, Virgil would have us see Aeneas as the vicarious source of destruction for Carthage as well as for its ruler.

We will soon turn to the moment in book 12 where Aeneas in actual fact instigates the ruination of Latinus's city and follow the parallels that Virgil draws there between Aeneas and the Pyrrhus of book 2. In book 12 it is Venus, the hero's "most beautiful mother"[93] as she is called by Virgil with some irony, who instigates his action. In conclusion, here let us turn back to book 2, to the event that follows upon the death of Priam, where Venus takes the opposite course and checks her son from violent action: Aeneas's contemplation of the killing of Helen. It is the first occasion where we witness Aeneas's anger in operation and its manifestation is particularly shocking for the very brutality of his thoughts.[94]

As he narrates the story to Dido, Aeneas, finding himself alone, sees Helen as she hides at the temple of Vesta. Out of fear for her life from both Greeks and Trojans, "she was sitting, hated, by the altars" (*aris invisa sedebat*, 2. 574). Aeneas's response to the sight is anger combined with the desire for revenge (575–76):

> exarsere ignes animo; subit ira cadentem
> ulcisci patriam et sceleratas sumere poenas.

Fires blazed up in my mind. Anger comes over me to avenge my falling fatherland and to extract punishment for crime.

After acknowledging that the punishing of a woman would not ennoble his reputation, nevertheless even at the end of his soliloquy the idea of vengeance remains paramount (586–87):

> '...animum...explesse iuvabit
> ultricis flammae et cineres satiasse meorum.'[95]

"It will delight me to glut my mind with avenging flame and gratify the ashes of my people."

Aeneas admits to the madness of his emotions and their ambition (588) —

> 'talia iactabam et furiata mente ferebar...'

"I was hurling out such words and was carried with my mind in a frenzy... —"

when Venus appears, restrains his hand, and comments immediately on what Aeneas, in his retelling of the event to Dido, has also realized (594–95):

> 'nate, quis indomitas tantus dolor excitat iras?
> quid furis?'

"My child, what enormous resentment rouses your unbridled anger? Why are you raging?"

Aeneas in retrospect comments on his own insanity. His mother picks up the notion of rage (*furis*), but glosses it with the words *dolor* and *ira*. His madness finds a fitting complement in the bitterness and anger that accompany it.[96]

The ancient scholiast avers that Virgil's executors deleted the passage for the reason that Aeneas himself adumbrates — that it is unseemly for our noble hero, progenitor of Rome, to be emotionally drawn to contemplate killing a woman. But the close reader of Virgil puts the scene into a larger drama that spans the epic. The words that Venus uses to describe her son's passionate response to the sight of Helen have much in common with the way Virgil's narrator has his readers sense the emotionality of Juno from the epic's onset. We hear five times of her anger in the initial segment of the book,[97] and at line 25 it is coupled with *dolor*:

> necdum etiam causae irarum saevique dolores
> exciderant animo.

Also the reasons for her wrath and her fierce resentment had not slipped from her mind.

From the beginning of the poem, Juno and the storm that incorporates her destructive emotionality set a pattern for a furious response to circumstance, usually the result of individual hurt, that goes against rational human conduct. It is just such conduct that Aeneas contemplates emulating as he ponders the killing of Helen from which Venus must physically hold him back.[98]

But we must be yet more particular. It is not only a woman but also a type of suppliant that Aeneas meditates killing. Helen is keeping guard at the temple of Vesta and sitting at the goddess's altars (*aris*), seeking shelter from the Greeks and in particular from Menelaus. We have witnessed something parallel in the book's preceding episode where Priam, Hecuba, and their daughters have taken refuge at an altar at the center of their palace.[99] Even though the old king responds to Pyrrhus's menace by futilely donning his armor, it is of his role as a suppliant that Priam reminds his killer. Unlike his son, Achilles, as Priam puts it, "blushed before the rights and trust of a suppliant" (*iura fidemque / supplicis erubuit*, 541–42). As if to emphasize the horror of the Greek's action, Aeneas tells of how Pyrrhus "dragged the trembling old man to the very altar" (*altaria ad ipsa trementem / traxit*) and slaughtered him there. Not only does Pyrrhus kill a suppliant, he does so as a form of human sacrifice.

Virgil is not quite ready to have his hero play the role of Pyrrhus. He saves its first direct manifestation, as we have seen, for the bout of fury on which Aeneas embarks in book 10 after the death of Pallas. But Aeneas's emotional reaction to the sight of Helen, and Venus's calming response to it, when taken together, as they should be, anticipate the end of the *Aeneid*. We will continue to focus on the epic's conclusion in the chapters that follow. Let us look here only at the relation between this moment in book 2 and the poem's final lines. There Virgil follows the narration in book 2, but in reverse order. As Aeneas is about to kill, Virgil reminds us of his mother's moderating intervention at the earlier moment. Venus, we recall, questioned the propriety of her son's rage (594–95):

> 'nate, quis indomitas tantus dolor excitat iras?
> quid furis?'

At the epic's end it is the narrator who reveals Aeneas's emotionality (12. 945–47):

> ille, oculis postquam saevi monimenta doloris
> exuviasque hausit, furiis accensus et ira
> terribilis....

He, after he had drunk in with his eyes the remembrance of his savage resentment and the spoils, set aflame by furies and terrifying in his wrath....

The second parallel to the Helen episode at the poem's conclusion takes us backward into the story of book 2 but forward in book 12. In both cases it is Aeneas who is speaking. In book 2, he is narrating to Dido but also voicing his own inner monologue (2. 575–76):

> '...subit ira cadentem
> ulcisci patriam et sceleratas sumere poenas.'

"Anger overcomes me to avenge my falling fatherland and to exact guilty punishment."

In book 12, he is addressing Turnus at his feet (12. 948–49):

> '...Pallas te hoc vulnere, Pallas
> immolat et poenam scelerato ex sanguine sumit.'

"Pallas, Pallas sacrifices you with this wound and exacts punishment from your guilty blood."

These are the only two instances in the poem where Virgil uses forms of *sceleratus*, *sumo*, and *poena* together. In each case we can debate the meaning of *sceleratus*. In the first we ask whether Aeneas is accusing Helen of committing a *scelus*, a wicked deed, and therefore is worthy of being killed, or accusing himself (as he tells the story to Dido) of being ready to act immorally, and therefore worthy of his mother's deterring hand. But it is the larger picture that Virgil would have us primarily contemplate. In book 2, Aeneas ponders killing a suppliant, but is held back by his mother. In book 12, there is no restraint. Turnus is a *supplex* (930), humbled and at Aeneas's mercy. That he kills in anger brings the emotional story full circle from book 2 to book 12, as Aeneas is allowed to yield to his passionate side and to kill his helpless victim.

The word *immolat* (949) makes it clear that Aeneas considers himself Pallas's surrogate in killing Turnus. It is also a reminder that Virgil has twice in book 10 used the word to refer to Aeneas striking his victims.[100] Turnus, as we have said, is the last in a row of human sacrifices offered by Aeneas in revenge for Pallas's death. In book 2, we watched how Virgil juxtaposes the episodes of Priam and Helen to illustrate the different exemplifications of behavior on the part of Pyrrhus and Aeneas, the one sacrificing a suppliant, the other curbed from so doing. At the poem's conclusion, Aeneas, as he had been in book 10, becomes Pyrrhus, now for one last, decisive, climactic moment. The Helen passage brilliantly initiates the progress that leads inexorably from one moment to the other by showing us the devastating possibilities open for Aeneas's vengeful anger, if it is allowed free range. Virgil chooses to end his epic with its final manifestation.

Next we will turn in more detail to the connection between Aeneas and the destruction of cities.

CHAPTER 4

Aeneas the City Destroyer

CATHNESS: Some say, he's mad; others, that lesser hate him,
Do call it valiant fury: but, for certain,
He cannot buckle his distemper'd cause
Within the belt of rule.

Shakespeare, *Macbeth*, Act V, Scene 2

A T LINE 499 OF BOOK 12, the narrator tells us that Aeneas "lets loose all the reins of his angers" (*irarum...omnis effundit habenas*). In the first scene in which he next appears he initiates the destruction of Latinus's city, spurred on by his "most beautiful mother" (*genetrix pulcherrima*).[101] It is a focal moment as the epic nears its end. We have seen Aeneas witness the ruin of Troy and vicariously cause the death of Dido and the collapse of Carthage. Now he himself at last bears direct responsibility for initiating the destruction of a city. Since the action is purely gratuitous — Virgil could have had his heroes commence their final duel without any interruptions — and since the event pulls together many themes that we have been tracing earlier, we will offer it close scrutiny.

Before we do so, however, it is best to turn back to book 7, where several of the motifs that culminate in the final book find their start. As we might expect, the seventh book, as the beginning of the epic's second half, has much in common with the poem's opening. Again, the Trojans are landing on a foreign shore where an unknown ruler must be courted and before whom Ilioneus once more is the spokesman as he was earlier before the queen of Carthage.[102] But on the new occasion a more menacing element enters the narrative. According to the narrator, the Trojans are now a "foreign army" (*advena...exercitus*) and they bring with them, to paraphrase lines 41–42, battle, wars, and deaths to impetuous kings.[103]

Virgil expands, and particularizes, this notion with the most extended description of an omen in the poem (7. 59–70):

> laurus erat tecti medio in penetralibus altis
> sacra comam multosque metu servata per annos,
> quam pater inventam, primas cum conderet arces,
> ipse ferebatur Phoebo sacrasse Latinus,
> Laurentisque ab ea nomen posuisse colonis.
> huius apes summum densae (mirabile dictu)
> stridore ingenti liquidum trans aethera vectae
> obsidere apicem, et pedibus per mutua nexis
> examen subitum ramo frondente pependit.
> continuo vates 'externum cernimus' inquit

> 'adventare virum et partis petere agmen easdem
> partibus ex isdem et summa dominarier arce.'

In the midst of the palace, in the lofty inner chambers, there was a laurel whose foliage was sacred, preserved in awe over many years, which after its discovery father Latinus himself was said to have dedicated to Phoebus, when he established his first citadels, and from it to have given the name Laurentes to his settlers. Wondrous to tell, a thick multitude of bees, traveling through the clear heavens with a mighty roar, occupied its highest peak, and with the feet of one another intertwined hung, a sudden swarm, from a leafy branch. Immediately the seer says: "We see a foreign man arrive and a troop from the same parts seek the same parts and lord it over the topmost citadel."

As we turn from the earlier lines to the omen, Virgil moves us easily from the *advena exercitus* to the more particular arrival of Aeneas (*adventare virum*) and from the Trojan army to the bees as a swarm (*examen*) that is also a battle line (*agmen*).[104] And the martial metaphors continue with *obsidere*, with the meaning "to occupy" but also "to besiege," and *dominarier*, "to rule" but also "to dominate by force." The seer's interpretation of the advent of the Trojans is not simply an arch manner of saying that their campaign will be victorious and that they will win the height of power. A particular *arx* is meant for their departure in defeat and an equally particular citadel for their final, power-laden control.

The laurel, "in the midst of the palace, in the lofty inner chambers," is a reminder of the laurel in the center of Priam's palace in book 2 (512–14):

> aedibus in mediis nudoque sub aetheris axe
> ingens ara fuit iuxtaque veterrima laurus
> incumbens arae atque umbra complexa penatis.

In the middle of the palace and underneath the open vault of heaven there was a huge altar and next to it a laurel of great age, leaning over the altar and embracing the household gods in its shade.

We move from Troy to Latium, from one aged king to another, from the center of one palace to that of another. The narrator does not go so far here as openly to predict that a doom parallel to that suffered by Priam's city will be endured by that of Latinus. But he offers us a hint of such an equation by twice reflecting the language of book 2 in 7. 59:

> laurus erat tecti medio in penetralibus altis...

The first reminiscence occurs at 2. 507–8, immediately preceding the description of laurel and altar, as Aeneas has us imagine what was before the old king's eyes:

> urbis uti captae casum convulsaque vidit
> limina tectorum et medium in penetralibus hostem...

When he saw the situation[105] of the captured city and doors of the palace torn up and the enemy in the midst of its inner chambers...

Aeneas resorts to the same language while describing his own home later in the book as he tries to persuade his father to leave Troy. While addressing Anchises, he also apostrophizes his mother (2. 664–67):

> 'hoc erat, alma parens, quod me per tela, per ignis
> eripis, ut mediis hostem in penetralibus...cernam?'

"Gracious mother, was this why you rescued me through weapons, through flames, that I might see the enemy in the midst of its inner chambers?"

What the parallels in language tell us is that the enemy is already within the gates, the arrival of the Trojan "bees" means control of the city but also its incipient ruin.

We soon learn that the palace of Latinus is at the peak of his city (*urbe... summa*, 7. 171). But the phrase *summa arce* in the prophet's prediction doesn't find its actual fulfillment until we reach book 12 as Aeneas sets about the destruction of Latinus's city. We have the word *arx* first in the words of Saces imploring Turnus to come to the aid of his troops (12. 653–56):

> 'Turne, in te suprema salus, miserere tuorum.
> fulminat Aeneas armis summasque minatur
> deiecturum arces Italum excidioque daturum,
> iamque faces ad tecta volant....'

"Turnus, our last hope lies in you. Take pity on your people. Aeneas thunders in arms, and threatens to hurl down the Italians' highest citadels, and give them to destruction. Already brands fly toward the houses...."

And, as Aeneas departs for the final confrontation, the narrator tells us that "he leaves behind the highest citadels" (*summas deserit arces*, 698). Aeneas is in command of the heights of the burning city as he hastens to the duel that concludes the poem.

Before we turn to the actual firing of the city, we should look also at the second, complementary omen that Latinus beholds (7. 71–80):

> praeterea, castis adolet dum altaria taedis,
> et iuxta genitorem astat Lavinia virgo,
> visa (nefas) longis comprendere crinibus ignem
> atque omnem ornatum flamma crepitante cremari,
> regalisque accensa comas, accensa coronam
> insignem gemmis; tum fumida lumine fulvo
> involvi ac totis Volcanum spargere tectis.
> id vero horrendum ac visu mirabile ferri:
> namque fore inlustrem fama fatisque canebant
> ipsam, sed populo magnum portendere bellum.

Moreover, while he sets the altars ablaze with holy torches and the maiden Lavinia stands next to her father, she seemed (the horror!) to catch fire in her long hair, and to burn with crackling flame in all her adornments, ablaze in her royal locks, ablaze in her brilliantly jeweled crown, then to be wreathed like smoke in lurid glare and to scatter fire throughout the palace. That was spoken of as a dread, amazing sight, for they prophesied that she herself would be glorious in reputation and fortune, but that for her people she boded a great war.

Once again, and in conjunction with the appearance of the bees, we think back to book 2, here to the omen of flames licking the brow of young Iulus (2. 679–91). We watch the crest of his head (*apex*, 683) at its peak (*summo de vertice*, 682), as well as his hair (*comas*, 684; *crinem*, 685). But on this occasion the fire is harmless (*innoxia*, 683) and holy (*sanctos*, 686). By contrast, Lavinia's flames seem all-consuming of her accoutrements and spread by her throughout the whole dwelling. Finally, this is the only occasion in Latin letters where the adjective *fumidus* is descriptive of a person. The war that Lavinia's omen portends, and whose destructiveness for a moment she herself incorporates, is to be strongly associated with smoke as well as fire.

So let us turn now to book 12 with the notions of smoke and fire in mind. As is regular in Virgil we find a mixture of the metaphoric and the realistic. We hear of burning in connection with Turnus on some half a dozen occasions. He burns (*ardet*: 12. 3) as his violence seizes him in its blaze (*accenso*, 9). The image soon reappears at 55 when Amata embraces him "on fire" (*ardentem*) and at 71 when his yearning for battle is again associated with burning (*ardet*). He calls on his spear to aid him in slaying the Aeneas he calls effeminate. The narrator comments on the *furiae* by which he is driven, but underscores the moment by a strong renewal of the fire image and a simile comparing Turnus's sheer animal force to a bull preparing to do battle (101–4):

> his agitur furiis, totoque ardentis ab ore
> scintillae absistunt, oculis micat acribus ignis,
> mugitus veluti cum prima in proelia taurus
> terrificos ciet atque irasci in cornua temptat.

He is driven by this madness, and from the whole of his blazing face sparks fly off, flame flashes from his fierce eyes, just as when a bull at the start of battle gives vent to fearful bellows and tries to throw anger into his horns.

When wounded Aeneas cedes from battle, his foe once again seethes with burning (*fervidus ardet*, 325), and, near the end, as he prepares to enter the final contest, a prey to "love driven by furies" (*furiis agitatus amor*, 668), he turns "the burning orbs of his eyes" (*ardentis oculorum orbis*, 670) toward the city that Aeneas is setting afire.

Likewise, the fire image continues brilliantly on, also associated with Lavinia and her famous blush as she responds to Amata's cautionary words to Turnus (64–66):

> accepit vocem lacrimis Lavinia matris
> flagrantis perfusa genas, cui plurimus ignem
> subiecit rubor et calefacta per ora cucurrit.

Lavinia listened to her mother's words, with her burning cheeks suffused with tears while a deep blush kindled its fire and ran across her glowing face.

The vividness of her response complements the corresponding inner fire on the part of her lover Turnus, and both anticipate the war that results from their interaction. But metaphor turns to reality at the only moment in book 12 where smoke companions fire, namely Aeneas's setting of the city of Latinus aflame. To this episode we must now turn (554–56):

> Hic mentem Aeneae genetrix pulcherrima misit
> iret ut ad muros urbique adverteret agmen
> ocius et subita turbaret clade Latinos.

> At this moment Aeneas's most beautiful mother put into his mind to advance on the walls and turn his forces toward the city and throw the Latins into turmoil with sudden disaster.

We note the presence of the *agmen* and the suddenness of the enterprise which is called to our attention twice again in the subsequent narration (*inceptum subitum*, 566; *subitus ignis*, 576). Both remind us of the omen of the bees while Lavinia's smoke and fire take tangible shape in the "smoking rooftops" (*fumantia culmina*, 569), which Aeneas threatens to level to the ground, and in the flames (*flammis*, 573) and fire (*ignis*, 576) by which the process begins.[106]

There are other details to which we should attend. One fact gives the moment a contemporary Roman tone. As Aeneas exhorts his troops forward to the destruction of the city he addresses them as "O citizens" (o *cives*, 572). The constitution of the invading Trojan army is suddenly said to be that of Roman citizens, obedient to the harangue of the leader in their midst. Virgil doesn't leave this striking moment without irony. As a result of the appearance of an army at the walls with ladders and fire — we will look at details in a moment — the narrator tells us (583–86):

> exoritur trepidos inter discordia civis:
> urbem alii reserare iubent et pandere portas
> Dardanidis ipsumque trahunt in moenia regem;
> arma ferunt alii et pergunt defendere muros,...

> Dissension arises among the fearful citizens: some bid to unbar the city and to open the gates to the Dardans, and drag the king himself to the walls; others bring arms and proceed to defend the walls,...

Virgil uses the abstraction *discordia*, in juxtaposition with *civis*, in his first eclogue (line 71) to signify civil war and what its horror ordains for the country's suffering citizenry. The destructive onslaught of Aeneas here foments a double form of internecine strife, first of citizen against citizen within Latinus's city, second of Aeneas's soldier-citizens against the inhabitants of an Italian town of which they should ideally be compatriots. We would not be wide of the mark in sensing the looming presence of Virgil's contemporary Rome, even of Octavian himself, in these proceedings.

To complicate matters still further is the image of Troy in the background. When hearing of the smoking *culmina* that Aeneas threatens to raze to the ground, we think of the *culmina* (2. 478) against which the Greeks are hurling flames, as he tells the story to Dido. Aeneas endured the destruction of his own native city and bore the unwitting responsibility for the suicide of the Carthaginian queen and for the doom of city "with the enemy let in" (*immissis hostibus*) and "raging flames rolling through the rooftops" (*flammae furentes culmina per...volvantur*).[107] He is now directly accountable for the initiation of a city's demise. But the poet gives a particular, immediate turn to the parallel between Troy and Latinus's city, and between the aged kings of each.

Virgil uses the phrase *primosque trucidant* (12. 577) only once elsewhere, at 2. 494, where the Greeks, the *immissi Danai*, break into the palace of Priam, slaughtering those who guard the doors. But Virgil's self-allusion grows more specific in what follows (12. 579–80):

> ipse inter primos dextram sub moenia tendit
> Aeneas, magnaque incusat voce Latinum...

> Aeneas himself among the first stretches out his hand beneath the walls, and with a loud voice reproaches Latinus...

The parallel moment in book 2 occurs at line 479 where Pyrrhus, also *ipse inter primos*, grabs a double-bladed axe and starts hacking down the doors of Priam's palace. We have seen how Virgil has been at pains to draw analogies between Aeneas and Achilles or his son Pyrrhus, and he offers here another striking example. Aeneas, witness earlier to the ruin of Troy and to Pyrrhus's gruesome killing of Priam, now initiates the firing of Latinus's city. Unlike Pyrrhus, however, Aeneas doesn't kill the city's old king (the hero's most striking act of bloodshed is saved for the epic's final moments). But, in drawing a further parallel here between Trojans and Greeks, and between Aeneas and Pyrrhus, Virgil once again reminds us of how, as he changes from powerless to powerful, Aeneas's actions tend toward imitating the more brutal deeds that he or his people have endured in the past. Witness to a city's ruin, city destroyer, and city founder are with some irony one and the same.

Book 12 contains the most similes of any book in the *Aeneid*. As always for Virgil any simile offers special clues to enable our readings of the text that it embellishes. Those of the epic's final book are especially privileged because not only do they help us to the deeper understanding of particular episodes, they also develop and bring to a climax motifs that Virgil has established at important moments earlier in the poem. The simile that concludes the initiation of the city's firing is no exception (12. 587–92). The Latins hasten to defend their ramparts:

> inclusas ut cum latebroso in pumice pastor
> vestigavit apes fumoque implevit amaro;
> illae intus trepidae rerum per cerea castra
> discurrunt magnisque acuunt stridoribus iras;
> volvitur ater odor tectis, tum murmure caeco
> intus saxa sonant, vacuas it fumus ad auras.

Just as when a shepherd has tracked bees enclosed in a crannied rock and filled them with bitter smoke. Frightened they rush around inside, through their waxen camp, and whet their wrath with loud buzzing. A black stench swirls within their dwellings. Then the rocks inside echo with dark rumble. The smoke makes its way to the empty breezes.

Virgil takes his start from a simile in the *Argonautica* of Apollonius Rhodius where Jason and his men scare off the Bebrycians (2. 130–34):

And as shepherds or beekeepers smoke out a great swarm of bees within a rock, and for a while the flustered bees stay together and buzz in their hive, but when suffocated by the smoke they dart forth far from the rock, likewise the men…(Race)

As he does regularly, Virgil would have us concentrate on the differences as well as the similarities between the two comparisons. We move from "shepherds or beekeepers" in Apollonius to Virgil's single shepherd who would not by profession be someone who has bees in his care. In Apollonius the bees buzz within their hive, and then escape from the rock after being smoked out. In Virgil, more ominously, only smoke makes its way into the open air, as if to say that the shepherd may be using his weapon solely for destructive purposes.

   Likewise Virgil asks us to take close notice of the interior of the bee-fortress and attend to the fear and anger of its denizens. We share in their reactions among other reasons because through the poet's magic we attend closely to both the smell and the noise involved through examples of synesthesia: the stench is black, like the means of its engendering, and the sound is equally dark and impenetrable, also because of the smoke. The Aeneas who earlier in the book had inveighed against *discordia* (313) and *iras* (314) now foments *discordia* (583) and *iras* (590) among the bee-Latins. Virgil also leaves clearly open the possibility that this shepherd has no concern for the survival of the creatures he is pursuing.[108] The poet also seems to have invented the phrase *vacua aura* here, furthering the implication that, as the result of the shepherd's efforts at fumigation, no bees escape from their hiding place to fill the air outside.[109] We are left to ask if the shepherd is simply inept, or does an element of deliberate cruelty enter into his behavior?

The simile also brings to a climax, and amalgamates, two themes that dot the epic at significant moments. The first concerns bees themselves. We have already analyzed the bee omen that initiates the narrative of book 7. But it is well to recall here the two previous similes where bees serve as comparanda. The first, which we also examined earlier, occurs at 1. 430–36, where the Carthaginians, at work on the construction of their new city, are compared to bees, "in the newness of summer" (*aestate nova*), going about their various tasks (436):

fervet opus redolentque thymo fragrantia mella.[110]

The work is intense, and the sweet-smelling honey reeks of thyme.

In other words, we are watching the happy spectacle of citizen-artisans as bees, working to bring productive order to their city at its foundation.

For the second bee simile we find ourselves in the Underworld, watching the countless souls that fly around the River Lethe (6. 707–9):

ac veluti in pratis ubi apes aestate serena
floribus insidunt variis et candida circum
lilia funduntur, strepit omnis murmure campus.

Just as when bees, in cloudless summer, settle upon colorful flowers and overspread the brilliant lilies, the whole plain resounds with the buzz.

As we turn from one simile to the other, we move from the start of summer to a serene summer day with bees swarming among the flowers that give them their livelihood. In the first we witness the creative progress of a new state under construction. In the second we enjoy the spectacle of souls poised to drink from the Lethe so that they can be reborn into the world of the living. In both instances, Aeneas is the viewer within the narrative. At the Carthaginians he marvels,[111] and after the simile exclaims on their good fortune. At the multitude of ghosts readied for a new life, he first simply watches (*videt*, 6. 703). Then, after the simile, a startled son asks his father as guide to expound the meaning of what he has beheld.

Returning to the simile of book 12 we find a different Aeneas from the protagonist of the two previous events. No longer is the hero watching in admiration and astonishment, as action happens around him that in the second instance needs explanation for him to understand. In book 12 he is the cause of the action that, by contrast with the other two situations, has a distinctly negative cast. Instead of marveling passively at the Carthaginian bees crafting their novel world, he now not only instigates dissension within an apiary community to become an armed camp, he also seems bent on its destruction, if we follow the poet's suggestiveness. We are no longer concerned with generation or glorying in the sheer joy of summer's day. Death, not birth, or rebirth, is apparently in the offing.

The history of shepherd similes strikes a parallel note. Once more there are also two predecessors to that of book 12. The first, mentioned briefly before, occurs in book 2 as Aeneas begins to apprehend the forces at work destroying his city. He stands, ears pricked up (304–8):

> in segetem veluti cum flamma furentibus Austris
> incidit, aut rapidus montano flumine torrens
> sternit agros, sternit sata laeta boumque labores
> praecipitisque trahit silvas; stupet inscius alto
> accipiens sonitum saxi de vertice pastor.

> Even as when with raging Southwinds a fire falls upon a corn crop, or a torrent rushing from a mountain river lays low fields, lays low lush seedlings and the efforts of cattle and drags forests headlong; a bewildered shepherd is stunned, listening to the sound from a rock's lofty crest.[112]

Virgil's source, as so often, is Homer, on this occasion *Iliad* 4. 452–55. In Homer, the clash of armies is compared to the noise of two rivers converging that a shepherd apprehends from a distant mountain:

As when rivers in winter spate running down from the mountains throw together at the meeting of streams the weight of their water out of the great springs behind in the hollow stream-bed, and far away in the mountains the shepherd hears their thunder.... (Lattimore)

As commentators note,[113] Virgil brings the shepherd forward into the narrative. It is on Aeneas — *pastor* is the simile's final word — and his ignorance of the destruction at hand that we finally attend as he embellishes his tale to Dido. He is the inert victim of violent circumstances which he appreciates only through hearing and over which he has no control.

But Virgil may be suggesting a further form of distance and consequently of lack of understanding. The landscape's order that the onslaught of nature demolishes is an addition to Homer by the Roman poet to suggest the civilizing that man brings to the crafting of his urban world.[114] In the simile such shaping is the work of a farmer, learned in georgic ways. The shepherd, as Aeneas sees and projects himself, might therefore appear doubly unknowing, first, of nature's negative handling of man's efforts at order, and second, of the particular details that might pattern the land itself.

Aeneas's ignorance is also a prominent detail in Virgil's second simile involving a shepherd (4. 69–73) as lovesick Dido roams her city:

> ...qualis coniecta cerva sagitta
> quam procul incautam nemora inter Cresia fixit
> pastor agens telis liquitque volatile ferrum
> nescius: illa fuga silvas saltusque peragrat
> Dictaeos; haeret lateri letalis harundo.

> ...like a deer off her guard, once the arrow has sped, whom an unwitting shepherd hunting with spears has pierced from a distance in the groves of Crete and has lodged the flying weapon. In flight she roams the forests and woodlands of Dicte. The deadly arrow clings to her side.

We will return to further aspects of this simile shortly. Suffice it to point out here a few salient details. In comparing the *pastor* of book 2 with that of book 4, we find that he still remains in ignorance of what has happened (*nescius*, which gains particular force here from its enjambment, carries much the same implications as *inscius*). Nevertheless, now he is an agent, the active cause, however innocent, of one of the epic's most tragic events. We know from the book's opening lines that Dido "nourishes with her veins the wound" by which she has been afflicted because of Aeneas's presence. The metaphoric lethal arrow will metamorphose, at the book's end, into the abandoning lover's real sword, the means by which the Carthaginian queen now deals herself the final deadly blow.

There is, however, a further parallel with the simile of book 2. Aeneas, *inscius pastor*, seems unconscious not only of the destructive force of fire and water but also of the order brought to the agricultural world by the work of farmers, a sphere of activity different from shepherding, as the Virgilian career illustrates in its progress from pastoral to georgic. Aeneas in book 4, as *pastor nescius* who is also a hunter, actively, if perhaps momentarily, pursues a career that would not be usual for one who was essentially a guardian of tame animals.[115] The hero, as unintentionally harmful lover, has strayed, it could be said, from the ordinary pastoralist's pacific realm into a more treacherous, threatening sphere of endeavor where deadly violence is the order of the day. He is not where he ought to be, with tragic results.

By the time we reach book 12 we find a *pastor* fully responsible for his deeds. Here, too, the shepherd's activity is encroaching on a province not usually his. (As we have seen, Virgil carefully suppresses Apollonius's beekeepers from his simile.) The professional apiculturalist, as we learn from *Georgic* 4, deliberately smokes out his charges to enforce their return to hive and honey-making. Virgil's final shepherd, by contrast, searches out bees in their hideaway of pumice with no positive purpose of which we are made aware. And the poet leaves us to speculate on whether or not any bees survived his barrage of smoke. If they did, the reader is not so informed.

I said earlier that, when Aeneas at last himself initiates the destruction of a city, the ruler doesn't actually die. Unlike Priam in book 2 and Dido in 4, king Latinus survives the conflagration to witness the final conflict between the two heroes (12. 707). Though strictly true, Virgil offers a variation on the theme in the episode immediately subsequent to the bee-shepherd simile by having the queen, Amata, commit suicide when she sees "the ramparts invaded, flames flying toward the roofs,"[116] and presumes that Turnus is dead. At the start of the book Virgil has been at pains to connect Amata with the queen of Carthage, and the episode of her suicide confirms the intimacy.[117] So, in fact, a surrogate Dido, equally a suicide, does die in connection with the burning of Latinus's city and Aeneas is again tangentially responsible. We never hear that the city was razed, nor does its ruler die, but the death of a principal character is still a striking part of the event.

First we note Amata's initial appearance in the book (54–57):

> At regina nova pugnae conterrita sorte
> flebat et ardentem generum moritura tenebat:
> 'Turne, per has ego te lacrimas, per si quis Amatae
> tangit honos animum....'

> But the queen, frightened by the new turn of the battle, was weeping and, readied for death, kept holding her impassioned son-in-law: "Turnus, I, you, by these tears, by any regard for Amata that might touch your heart...."

Dido permeates these lines. The words *At regina* at the start of an hexameter are a signpost for three prominent turns of event in the fourth book (1, 296, 504). *Moritura* both recalls Dido's initial resolution to die (4. 308) and anticipates Amata's death scene (12. 602). And the language of oaths with which she begins her plea to the man she wishes to be her son-in-law parallels that which Dido employs when first addressing her departing lover (4. 314, 316):

> '...per ego has lacrimas dextramque tuam te...
> per conubia nostra, per inceptos hymenaeos....'

> "I, you, by these tears and your right hand...by our wedding, by the marriage upon which we entered...."

Her very name Amata, "the loved one," as well as the narrator's pronouncement in book 7 that she yearned "with an astonishing love" (*miro amore*, 57) for Turnus to marry her daughter may account for her emotionality here. It also goes some distance to explain her Dido-like suicide. There are also further parallels: Amata looks out from her palace on the scene below (*tectis prospicit*, 595) just as the queen of Carthage views the departure of the Trojans (*prospiceres arce ex summa*, 4. 410).[118] *Infelix*, her prominent characteristic at 598, is an adjective that Virgil allots Dido on eight occasions. The response to her death (607–8)

> ...resonant late plangoribus aedes.
> hinc totam infelix vulgatur fama per urbem....

> The palace resounds far and wide with lamentation. From here the wretched rumor is broadcast through the whole city....

corresponds to that of Carthage, as we saw, at Dido's demise (4. 666–68):

> ...concussam bacchatur fama per urbem.
> lamentis gemituque et femineo ululatu
> tecta fremunt, resonat magnis plangoribus aether....

Rumor rushes wildly through the stricken city. The houses resound with lamentations, and moaning and the keening of women, the heavens reecho with great wailing....

As Dido is one with Carthage, and her death implies its ruin, so Virgil implicates Amata with the Latin city. Just as Aeneas's goal is to "confound the Latins with sudden disaster" (*subita turbaret clade Latinos*, 556), so she decides on self-slaughter "when confounded in her mind by sudden anguish" (*subito mentem turbata dolore*, 599).[119] And as Aeneas styles the city as "this source...this center of a wicked war" (*hoc caput...haec belli summa nefandi*, 572), so Amata accuses herself of being "the reason, and the guilt, and the source of evil" (*se causam...crimenque caputque malorum*, 600). At the conclusion of the episode the narrator suggests an association of the two events by Latinus (609–10):

> ...it scissa veste Latinus
> coniugis attonitus fatis urbisque ruina,...

Latinus makes his way, garments rent, dazed by the doom of his wife and destruction of his city,...

We will look in the next chapter at one further, subsequent analogy between the closing moments of the *Aeneid* and the death of Dido, namely the departure from the narrative of Juturna, Turnus's sister, an immortal version of the queen's mortal sister, Anna. All three events — the initiation of the city's burning, the suicide of Amata, and the forced retreat of Juturna from the action — are superfluous interruptions to the inexorable progress of the narrative toward the final clash. They add poignancy in abundance but do not advance the action. Yet on another, allegorical level they are cumulative and form a further powerful history of emotionality that leads with equal directness to the ending. Turnus is a Dido figure at the start of the final book and at its conclusion. In between we recapitulate versions of the destruction of Carthage, the death of Dido, and the abandonment of Anna. The main difference, as we have said, is that Turnus's death is not a suicide but now directly caused by Dido's former lover, the ancestral founder of Rome.

Let us conclude by looking at another of the extraordinary similes from book 12 that pulls together and brings to a climax motifs prominent earlier in the epic. The city is on fire. Now the chase begins in earnest, with Aeneas as hounding dog, Turnus as frightened deer (12. 749–55):

> inclusum veluti si quando flumine nactus
> cervum aut puniceae saeptum formidine pennae
> venator cursu canis et latratibus instat;
> ille autem insidiis et ripa territus alta
> mille fugit refugitque vias, at vividus Umber
> haeret hians, iam iamque tenet similisque tenenti
> increpuit malis morsuque elusus inani est.

As when a hunter hound has caught a stag penned in by a stream or hedged about through fear of crimson feathers and presses after him with a rush, barking. The stag, frightened by the snares and the high bank, runs a thousand ways to and fro in flight, but the eager Umbrian grabs at him with gaping jaws, and now, even now, holds him, or, as if he were holding him, snaps his teeth, deceived with an empty mouthful.

We first meet Aeneas the hunter in book 1, sighting deer (*cervos*, 184) and "pursuing them with spears" (*agens telis*, 191) in order to feed his followers. Literal turns metaphoric when the phrase *agens telis* reappears at line 71 of book 4 during the simile I quoted earlier where Aeneas is compared to a shepherd who has unwittingly shot a doe with a deadly arrow. Already from the initial lines of the book we have learned of Dido's wound and of how she fosters it. The simile brings Aeneas as the wound's inflictor directly into the picture. The next scene returns us to the world of actual hunting. Venus first announces her plan to Juno that the next day (4. 117–18):

> 'venatum Aeneas unaque miserrima Dido
> in nemus ire parant....'

"Aeneas and Dido, most lovesick, make ready to enter the forest on the hunt...."

At dawn we hear of the preparations, of hunting spears (*venabula*, 131) and of dogs who make their first, striking appearance in the poem through their keen sense of smell (*odora canum vis*, 132).[120] Again, there is an intermingling of literal and figurative. Death to animals is the purpose of the hunt — Iulus is bent on tracking a boar or a lion — but it is in fact the death of Dido that is in the offing as its result (169–70):

> ille dies primus leti primusque malorum
> causa fuit.

That day was the initial cause of death, the initial cause of evil.

And Aeneas as well as the day, Aeneas, first shepherd-hunter, now Apollo in simile, is also the cause (143–44, 147–49):

> qualis ubi hibernam Lyciam Xanthique fluenta
> deserit ac Delum maternam invisit Apollo....
> ipse iugis Cynthi graditur mollique fluentem
> fronde premit crinem fingens atque implicat auro,
> tela sonant umeris.

> Just as when Apollo leaves behind Lycia in winter and the streams of Xanthus and visits his mother's Delos.... He himself treads the ridges of Cynthus and with soft foliage fashions and binds his flowing hair and entwines it with gold. On his shoulders arrows rattle.

Critics rightly juxtapose this simile with that in book 1, where Dido is likened to Apollo's twin sister Diana, also, among other specifics, enjoying the ridges of Mount Cynthus (*iuga Cynthi*, 1. 498). But one detail that Virgil places prominently at the end of the Apollo simile sets the two apart. The picture of arrows rattling on the god's shoulders is drawn from *Iliad* 1. 46, where he descends as plague-bringer upon the Greeks. Aeneas-Apollo's weapons do not yet carry literal death to the queen of Carthage, but the hunter, whether a human shepherd or the god of the bow and the lyre, has already stalked his doomed prey.

Book 7, as we have seen, often lays the groundwork for aspects of the poem that culminate in book 12. Here it serves as transition. At the instigation of Juno, in a series of episodes that balance the storm-scene of book 1, the fury Allecto maddens first Amata and her fellow mothers, then Turnus, into a desire for war. Her third victim is Iulus, who is again hunting (*venantis*, 493) and the nostrils of whose dogs she touches "with a scent they knew" (*noto odore*, 480). The result is that (7. 481–82):

...quae prima laborum
causa fuit belloque animos accendit agrestis.

...this was the first cause of the tribulations and fired the minds of
the country folk for war.

Instead of an anticipation of the death of Dido, hunting, like the omen
of bees and fire earlier in the book, now foresees the war to come with its
plethora of deaths. Yet Dido herself is also not far off.

The victim here is one of Virgil's greatest inventions, a stag tamed by
Silvia to become akin to a human sharing in her domestic life. The beast
is a fit symbol for the Italian landscape, and its docility a moving reflection of a world of communities "tranquil through length of peace" (*longa
placidas in pace*, 7. 46) before the arrival of the Trojans and their army.[121]
Nevertheless, this is not the first deer to which Virgil has introduced us.
We have seen Aeneas, literal deer driver in book 1, become symbolic deer-
stalker and wounder in book 4. We will see him in the next chapter as
symbolic hunter and predator, attacking Turnus as lion wounded in the
Punic fields, in the powerful simile that opens book 12.

As we move within book 12 from Turnus as Dido-lion to Turnus as Di-
do-deer, we share in the debilitating process that the poem's vanquished
hero undergoes as the book unfolds, from king of beasts to frightened
stag. The phrase *movet arma* of the opening simile, as we will see, yields
to the penned stag, frozen into terrified immobility.[122] Turnus's metamorphosis from lion to deer, which is to say from the height of courage
to the incorporation of pusillanimity, is paralleled by Aeneas's debase-
ment from human to animal, from hunter in the first simile to dog in
the second.[123] The choice is purposeful. Iulus's hounds begin the war by
pursuing Silvia's tamed stag which their master then wounds. Iulus's father, in Virgil's masterful telling, now absorbs their purpose as he tracks
down and pens in Turnus, the terrified deer. As *vividus Umber* Aeneas is
the landscape's new vital force.

One detail deserves further mention. The only other occasion in the
poem where Virgil uses the phrase *iam iamque* with a form of *teneo* is at
2. 529–30, where Pyrrhus pursues Polites to the feet of his father Priam:

...illum ardens infesto vulnere Pyrrhus
insequitur, iam iamque manu tenet et premit hasta.

Pyrrhus ablaze pursues him with hostile wound, and now, even now,
clutches him with his hand and presses him with his spear.

We have seen Aeneas as Pyrrhus as he initiates the destruction of Latinus's city. He is Achilles's son yet again now as he brings to bay his terrified quarry. The arc from Dido as deer to Turnus as deer, and from Aeneas as unwitting shepherd to Aeneas as aggressive hound assailing his prey reaches its end only as the poem itself verges toward its conclusion.

In the next chapter we turn to Aeneas's primary antagonist, Turnus, and to the authority with which Virgil invests him as the epic draws toward closure.

CHAPTER 5

The Authority of Turnus

...And if He pauses? If His sword hovers above

Your chest? Here's where you tear a hole in the poem,
a hole in the mind, here's where the russet glare
of ships aflame and the pyre and the amethyst gleam
from the boy's sword belt rise and roil in a blur.

We are trapped in meanings that circulate like blood.
The sword descends. And He who kills you is not
a myth, nor a city. His eyes searching yours could
be a lover's eyes. It was love He fought.

Rosanna Warren, "Turnus," from *Departures* (2003)

VIRGIL BEGINS AND ENDS the final book of the *Aeneid* with Turnus, first with his apprehension of future doom, then with his death.[124] He fixes the initial moment in the reader's mind with one of his most extraordinary similes (12. 4–8):

> ...Poenorum qualis in arvis
> saucius ille gravi venantum vulnere pectus
> tum demum movet arma leo, gaudetque comantis
> excutiens cervice toros fixumque latronis
> impavidus frangit telum et fremit ore cruento.

> Just as in Punic fields a lion, stricken by hunters with a grievous wound in the chest, then at last goes to battle and, joyfully tossing his flowing mane from his neck, without fear breaks the robber's embedded arrow and roars with bloody mouth.

Homeric heroes in the heat of the fray are often compared to lions, and Turnus himself, battling the Trojans, has already been allotted such a comparison in book 9.[125] But Virgil calls the analogy especially to our attention not only from its unusual placement near the start of the book but also by turning what we expect to be a literal comparison into a metaphysical one. This lion is suffering a spiritual, not a physical hurt. A brigand (*latro*), one of a group of hunters (*venantum*), has launched an attack upon the beast, which means, in the case of Aeneas as hunter-robber, someone who is about to deprive him of land and love. He therefore arouses an appropriate emotional response.

The lion Turnus is fearless in response, but the final words of the simile add another characteristic. *Fremit ore cruento* is the concluding phrase of a second lion simile in book 9 (339–41), where the overwrought slaughter of Nisus and Euryalus is brought vividly before the reader.[126] But a still earlier use of the words illustrates more directly Turnus's inner rage and lends it a further resonance. *Fremet...ore cruento* is the expression that Virgil places in Jupiter's mouth in book 1 (296) to describe the appearance of *Furor impius*, the monstrous figuration of civil war that, we are told, will come to an end under the new dispensation of Augustus.

Turnus's rage is notorious. *Violentia*, for instance, is a characteristic given by Virgil only to him. And the various forms the hero's fury takes will continue on in book 12, even as hope for his survival recedes.[127] At 668 we hear of his "love harried by furies" (*furiis agitatus amor*) and shortly later he will ask of his sister Juturna (680), in anticipation of his demise:

> '...hunc, oro, sine me furere ante furorem.'

> "I pray you, let me first rage forth this rage."

But Virgil gives a particular twist to Turnus's bloody-mouthed roaring by the connection with Jupiter's *Furor impius*. In a response to Turnus's initial request to Latinus that a treaty be prepared for settlement of the war by single combat with Aeneas, the old king urges calm on his would-be son-in-law.[128] But in the process he says of himself (12. 29–31):

> 'victus amore tui, cognato sanguine victus
> coniugis et maestae lacrimis, vincla omnia rupi;
> promissam eripui genero, arma impia sumpsi.'

> "Overcome by affection for you, overcome by kindred blood and the tears of the sorrowing queen, I broke all bonds; I snatched the betrothed from my son-in-law, I took up impious arms."

Turnus's emotionality has the result of driving Latinus to resort to warfare that pits brother against brother. The hero's action in engaging the Trojans in combat, as Virgil would have us understand it, smacks of civil strife, which the old king now realizes that he has abetted.

There is, however, a further dimension to the simile that both complements and challenges what it has already told us. Line 5 —

> saucius ille gravi venantum vulnere pectus —

is a careful reminder of the opening lines of book 4:

> At regina gravi iamdudum saucia cura
> vulnus alit venis et caeco carpitur igni.

> But the queen, now long stricken by grievous care, nourishes the wound with her veins and is seized by dark fire.

Just as we are reminded of Dido on several occasions during the opening scenes of book 11, so it is in the figure of Turnus that the presence of the Carthaginian queen is felt yet again. The simile is set "in the fields of the Carthaginians," and it is of her that Virgil would have us closely think. The metaphorical wound that Dido suffers at the opening of book 4 will soon also become real as, at the book's conclusion, she commits suicide with the sword of her lover, Aeneas, after his departure. Turnus's inner hurt stems from the diminution of his power and the robbery of Lavinia, at least in his eyes, by the marauding Trojans and their lord. But in this instance, as we turn from the beginning of the book to its finale (which is also the finale of the epic), Aeneas is the actual killer, the perpetrator now in fact of the fatal wound. In the first simile of book 4, we remember, Aeneas is compared to a shepherd on the hunt who leaves a deadly arrow in the side of a doe. The deer is "off her guard" (*incautam*, 4. 70) and the shepherd is "unaware" (*nescius*, 72) of what he has done. At the end of the poem there is no ignorance on the part of the killer. Aeneas bears direct responsibility for the death that brings his epic to its abrupt but powerful conclusion.

The leap from the book's beginning to its end is not as sudden as it may at first seem for the presence of Dido permeates the whole. We have looked earlier at one major reappearance of the Carthaginian queen, the suicide of Amata, in connection with discussion of Virgil's portrayal of Aeneas during the course of its narrative. Here I would like only to call attention to the other, most immediate, reminder of Dido, namely the final departure of Turnus's sister Juturna from the action. This occurs after Juturna has recognized the shriek of the Fury sent by Jupiter, on the surface to force her from the action, more deeply to signify her brother's inescapable doom.

Virgil emphasizes the connection of Juturna with Anna by repeating line 673 of book 4 near the beginning of the description (12. 871):

> unguibus ora soror foedans et pectora pugnis...

> her/his[129] sister, mutilating her features with her nails and her breast with blows...

The parallel persists in the opening lines of the two subsequent speeches directed by sibling to sibling. In book 4, it is Anna who addresses her dying sister (4. 675):

> 'hoc illud, germana, fuit? me fraude petebas?'

"Was this what it was, my sister? Were you seeking me in deceit?"

And as Juturna reluctantly prepares to abandon her doomed brother, she too begins with direct address (12. 872):

'quid nunc te tua, Turne, potest germana iuvare?'

"How, Turnus, can your sister now be of help to you?"

The combination of apostrophe — sister to sister, sister to brother — with the repetition of *germana* further unites the situations.[130] Finally, the rhetoric of the two speeches as wholes is built around an assemblage of interrogatives as each protagonist attempts to come to terms with her lot.

The placement of both episodes is crucial to our understanding of Virgil's art. In book 4, sister is bidding farewell to dying sister. In book 12, sister is uttering her final words to a brother shortly to suffer death. We move from Turnus, metaphorically wounded by someone who is both hunter and despoiler, to Turnus killed at last by his enemy, Aeneas. And the person of Dido, figuratively injured by love's and a lover's hurts and who then becomes a literal suicide from the same source, looms behind both events. In book 4, Aeneas is the unwitting cause of Dido's doom. In book 12, in the climactic manifestation of his own decisive emotionality, he is the direct cause of his victim's demise.[131]

To watch the dramatic change in Turnus, and in Virgil's treatment of him from the start of the book to its conclusion, as he gradually loses the support of those who have valued him[132] and gains the enmity of Jupiter whose negativity is at the last incorporated in Aeneas,[133] we must turn back to the opening simile and to the word *impavidus*. In spite of his inner pain, Turnus presents himself to his immediate world as fearless. It is a characteristic that Virgil emphasizes during his *aristeia* following upon the wounding of Aeneas. Take the simile at 12. 331–36, comparing him to the god of war:

> qualis apud gelidi cum flumina concitus Hebri
> sanguineus Mavors clipeo increpat atque furentis
> bella movens immittit equos, illi aequore aperto
> ante Notos Zephyrumque uolant, gemit ultima pulsu
> Thraca pedum circumque atrae Formidinis ora
> Iraeque Insidiaeque, dei comitatus, aguntur....

Like bloody Mars when, roused along the waters of the chill Hebrus, he clashes his shield and, setting out for war, drives on his raging steeds: they fly ahead of South Winds and West on the open plain, farthest Thrace groans from the thud of feet, and around him the figure of black Fear, and Angers and Ambushes, attendants of the god, rush forward....

The simile is drawn from *Iliad* 13. 298–303, where Idomeneus in battle is compared to Ares who is accompanied by his son Rout. Virgil is more elaborate. He brings before us not only the explicit location but the sheer energy of the war god and his horses. Homer's Rout is expanded by the later poet into Angers, Deceits, Terror. It is especially the latter, the Fear that is part of the retinue of Turnus-Mars, that claims our attention. In terms of the simile's rhetoric, its lack of parallel with its colleagues *Iraeque Insidiaeque* makes it stand out as well as the fact that the phrase *atrae Formidinis ora* is drawn directly from Lucretius.[134]

We will return shortly to the poet of *De Rerum Natura* for elucidation of this passage and for his continued force at the conclusion of the book. What Virgil would have us observe here is the presence of Fear as an abstraction that Turnus, for a moment in the ascendant, instills in others. As the book's peripeteia evolves, however, he experiences, rather than inflicts, fear as well as anger and treachery. For *formido* I think particularly of the striking use of the noun during the simile at 749–55 where, we recall, Turnus is compared to a deer "hemmed in by fear of crimson feathers" (*puniceae saeptum formidine pennae*, 750). *Formido* is the technical term for a rope decorated with brilliant feathers used by hunters to frighten animals. But, in the case of Turnus, it is the abstract Fear, something he must now endure rather than impose on others, that remains as important as the tangible object that implants the terror.

The association of Turnus with fear continues to the poem's end. Not long after the deer simile we learn that Turnus was "out of his mind from fear" (*amens formidine*, 776), and, as he recognizes the sound of the Fury sent by Jupiter to terrify both sister and brother (867):

> illi membra novus solvit formidine torpor....[135]

a new numbness slackens his limbs from fear....

Turnus as *sanguineus Mavors*, spattered with the blood on which war battens, gives place to the hero's chill blood that tautens with cold as the end approaches (*gelidus concrevit frigore sanguis*, 905).[136] The *Insidiae* who accompany Turnus-Mars as he goes into battle become the *insidiis* (752) that Turnus now experiences as frightened stag. Virgil saves *Irae* for Aeneas himself as, "terrifying in his wrath" (*ira terribilis*, 946–47), he prepares to give his victim the death blow. Once again, and for a final time, the anger that Turnus brings with him as he goes to war is turned against him in the person of terror-inspiring, fury-driven Aeneas.

The association of cold with fear prepares us for one of the major role-reversals of the poem. At line 92 of the epic's first book, in the midst of Juno's destructive storm, we are told that "Aeneas's limbs are slackened from chill" (*Aeneae solvuntur frigore membra*). By the time we reach the concluding lines of the poem, as the final anxiety for imminent death comes upon him, it is Turnus's limbs which are slackened from cold (*ast illi solvuntur frigore membra*, 12. 951). It is now the turn of the victim of a goddess's anger and resentment to become himself furious and to kill someone who is in a position parallel to that which had once been his. As the epic comes full circle, Aeneas can in fact take the life of the suppliant before him when earlier the angry queen of heaven had been incapable of fulfilling her vengeance.

Nor must we forget the presence of Dido at this moment when Virgil centers so much from his past narrative. The ruler of Carthage commits self-slaughter "inflamed by a sudden fury" (*subito...accensa furore*, 4. 697), and Aeneas is only vicariously accountable. By the time we reach the end, Aeneas is made to take explicit responsibility as "set aflame by furies" (*furiis accensus*, 12. 946)[137] he takes the life of his humbled opponent.

Let me offer one further example of how, as his epic concludes, Virgil makes us see Turnus as an earlier Aeneas who is challenged by a stronger power. For this we must look back once more to the *Iliad*.

Turnus makes a single final, futile gesture of opposition to his foe as the end approaches. At line 896, the Rutulian sees a huge stone that serves as a boundary mark to prevent disputes (899–900):

> vix illum lecti bis sex cervice subirent,
> qualia nunc hominum producit corpora tellus.

Twelve chosen men, men of such physique as the earth now brings forth, might scarcely lift it on their neck.

Several of the motifs Virgil uses are drawn from Homer. Athena wields a stone that had served as a boundary mark in her fight with Ares (*Il.* 21. 403–6), and the theme of human physical decline recurs three times. In its simplest form we find it at 12. 445–50, where Hector employs a boulder to break open the gates of Troy. Homer treats it with more elaboration twice elsewhere, at 5. 302–6, where Diomedes heaves a rock against Aeneas (who escapes with the help of Aphrodite and Apollo), and at 20. 285–87, where Aeneas heaves a rock against Achilles. It is noteworthy that Aeneas appears in both the latter passages, but the second has particular bearing on Virgil's epic as it nears its end and as all strength vanishes from Aeneas's opponent (903–7):

> sed neque currentem se nec cognoscit euntem
> tollentemve manu saxumve immane moventem;
> genua labant, gelidus concrevit frigore sanguis.
> tum lapis ipse viri vacuum per inane volutus
> nec spatium evasit totum neque pertulit ictum.[138]

But he doesn't recognize himself, neither as he runs nor as he moves, as he lifts the huge stone or sets it in motion. His knees buckle, and his chill blood tautened with cold. Then the stone itself, whirled by him through the empty space, did not cover the whole distance or carry home its blow.

We have already mentioned the intimacy of cold with terror, and we will shortly examine in more detail the symptoms of fright that Virgil brilliantly conveys here by his use of slowing spondees and by the dull rote of repetitiveness that turns distinctions into similarities. But it is the thematic parallelism with the conflict between Achilles and Aeneas in *Iliad* 20 that deserves noting. By bringing it to bear on the *Aeneid*'s conclusion, Virgil furthers our association of Aeneas with Achilles and at the same time allusively equates Turnus with Homer's Aeneas at the moment when he does battle with the greatest of the Achaeans. Aeneas escapes with his life through the intervention of Poseidon just as Aeneas, at the opening of Virgil's epic, narrowly avoids death because Neptune calms the storm his sister Juno has stirred up. At the end of the poem Turnus-Aeneas is not so lucky. No divinity steps in now to avert his doom from a Turnus who brings with him the poetic legacy not only of Hector and Dido but of earlier Aeneases, both in Homer and in Virgil, who are luckier than Turnus.

There are two further items to be added to the list of changes in Turnus as we move from the beginning of book 12 to the end. Immediately before the Mars simile and just after Turnus learns of Aeneas's wounding, Virgil describes him as follows (325–27):

...subita spe fervidus ardet;
poscit equos atque arma simul, saltuque superbus
emicat in currum.

He burns, blazing with a sudden hope. He demands horses and weapons together, and in pride with a leap springs into his chariot.

Two adjectives are worth particular notice. The first is *fervidus*. Here,
while he is in glory, the attribute belongs to Turnus, but as the book
progresses and the hero's fortunes are reversed, the characterization becomes thriceover that of Aeneas. At 748, about to become the hunter-
hound in pursuit of Turnus as deer, Aeneas is *fervidus*. The adjective is
given by Turnus to Aeneas's words (*fervida dicta*) at 894–95. Finally, it
is as *fervidus* that Virgil describes Aeneas in the next to last line of the
poem. Enjambment gives the word great force as it delineates the warrior's fiery, ultimate appearance in the poem.

Secondly, we should take due note of the adjective *superbus*. We have
already seen how Virgil makes the characteristic of pride an emphatic
part of his depiction of Turnus by applying it to him, in one of his rare examples of second-person apostrophe, after he has killed Pallas (*te, Turne,
superbum*, 10. 514). It is appropriate that Virgil recall both the qualifica-
tion, and its appearance in book 10, here in the epic's concluding narrative, when Turnus is in power for a final moment. In this case, the poet
doesn't transfer the adjective to Aeneas as he does in the case of *fervidus*.
Instead, he applies its opposite, *humilis*, to Turnus, now a humbled suppliant at Aeneas's feet, asking forbearance of him (12. 930).

In summary, as we look ahead from the opening lines and the Mars
simile to the poem's ending, in the figure of the doomed hero we move
from Dido wounded to Dido killed, from Turnus terrifying to Turnus
terror-stricken, from Turnus haughty to Turnus abased. Meanwhile, the
anger that accompanies Turnus as he readies for battle becomes an attribute of Aeneas, as does the adjective *fervidus*. This epithet belongs to
Turnus when he is in power, but Virgil allots it to Aeneas at the moment
of closure as he furiously kills his pleading victim.

The next simile allotted to Turnus helps us formulate another equally
important metamorphosis. As he continues on his spate of killing, Virgil
compares him to a force of nature (12. 365–67):

ac velut Edoni Boreae cum spiritus alto
insonat Aegaeo sequiturque ad litora fluctus,
qua venti incubuere, fugam dant nubila caelo....

Just as when the blast of the Edonian North Wind roars over the depths of the Aegean and pursues the waves toward the shore, where the winds have born down, the clouds in the sky take to flight....

The inspiration for the simile lies with *Iliad* 11. 305–8, where Hector is doing battle:

And just as when the West Wind drives the clouds of the white South Wind, striking them with a violent squall, and many a swollen wave rolls onward, and on high the spray is scattered by the blast of the wandering wind, just so many heads of men were laid low by Hector.

In Homer the emphasis is on the number of Hector's victims. In Virgil we attend largely to the idea of flight and pursuit. The blast of the wind chases the floods (*sequitur*), the clouds attempt to escape (*fugam dant*). Virgil will vary the motif in the narrative and similes that follow and gradually reverse its implications. At line 615 Turnus still pursues (*sequitur*), but he is now more worn out (*segnior*). In the simile of 715–22, he is still one of two bulls fighting for control of his domain, but already at 645 he is in flight (*fugientem*). Both noun (*fuga*) and verb (*fugit*) recur at 733, and the noun appears again at 742 when Turnus discovers the futility of his sword. The subsequent simile where he is compared to the stag at bay shows escape as equally futile (*mille fugit refugitque vias*) and the notion spills over into the following narrative (*fugiens*).[139]

But Virgil has a further point in alluding to the simile of *Iliad* 11. He draws a comparison between Turnus, holding the field while the wounded Aeneas momentarily retreats, and Hector at one of the moments in the epic where he is most in control of his destiny. As the epic draws to a close matters are reversed. Turnus still remains a Hector figure but he is now at the mercy of Jupiter's Fury and of Aeneas, just as the Trojan hero yields his life to the best of the Achaeans during their conflict in *Iliad* 22. Virgil deepens his reader's understanding of the moment with one of his most extraordinary similes, the last of any length in the epic (12. 908–14):

ac velut in somnis, oculos ubi languida pressit
nocte quies, nequiquam avidos extendere cursus
velle videmur et in mediis conatibus aegri
succidimus; non lingua valet, non corpore notae
sufficiunt vires nec vox aut verba sequuntur:
sic Turno, quacumque viam virtute petivit,
successum dea dira negat.

As in dreams, when by night languid sleep weighs down the eye, we seem to desire in vain to pursue our eager course and in the midst of the endeavor, fainting, we fail; the tongue has no strength, the body does not furnish its usual power; neither voice nor words follow: thus wherever he valiantly sought escape, the dread goddess denied Turnus success.

We are now also with Achilles and Hector in conflict beneath the walls of Troy (*Iliad* 22. 199–201):

And as in a dream a man cannot pursue one who flees before him — the one cannot flee, nor the other pursue —

Homer's analogy depicts, in a nightmare, the impossibility of pursuit and capture as well as the impossibility of escape. Achilles nearly wins the day but not quite, since Apollo intervenes one last time to help the Trojan warrior. For Virgil, fashioning the last moments of Turnus, the question of pursuit, flight, and capture is no longer open. The chase has come to an end. We concentrate now solely on Turnus-Hector and his inability to move, which is to say, his powerlessness.

Virgil's lexical usage helps convey the special distinctiveness of the moment for us. These are the only uses of the phrases *mediis conatibus* and *notae vires* in preserved classical Latin. *Lingua valet* appears only here in poetry.[140] The expression *languida quies* is invented by Virgil and varied by Statius as is *avidos cursus*.[141] The words *nec vox aut verba sequuntur* are equally novel, to be imitated by Ovid and again Statius.[142] Virgil has the expression *oculos pressit* at *Aeneid* 9. 487, where Euryalus's mother bewails her inability to close the eyes of her son in death as part of his funeral rites (*nec...pressi oculos*). His use of the parallel phrase here in simile is a clear prelude to the arrival of the final *quies* of death for Turnus.[143]

The word *succidimus* deserves special consideration. One of its rare pre-Virgilian uses occurs in a passage in Lucretius on Virgil's mind as he elaborates the symptoms of Turnus's helplessness. In book 3, lines 152–58, of *De Rerum Natura*, the didactic poet is expounding the symptoms of fear:

> verum ubi vementi magis est commota metu mens,
> consentire animam totam per membra videmus
> sudoresque ita palloremque exsistere toto
> corpore et infringi linguam vocemque aboriri,
> caligare oculos, sonere auris, succidere artus,

denique concidere ex animi terrore videmus
saepe homines.

Nevertheless, when the understanding is stirred by some stronger fear, we see that the whole soul feels with it throughout the limbs, and then sweat and pallor break out over all the body, and the tongue is crippled and the voice is choked, the eyes grow misty, the ears ring, the limbs give way beneath us, and indeed we often see men fall down through the terror in their mind.[144] (Bailey)

Words such as *oculus*, *lingua*, *corpus*, and *vox* are in common between Lucretius and Virgil's simile, but the parallel usage by the two poets of *succidere/succidimus* has particular resonance.[145] The collapse of Turnus's limbs in fainting, within the dream simile, anticipates the reality of his knees doubling under him after his initial wounding by Aeneas (*duplicato poplite*, 927). By themselves the symptoms of fear, as clinically detailed by Lucretius and echoed in Virgil's analogy, simply bring to a climax the terror that has gripped Turnus since the direct confrontation between him and Aeneas began. We earlier observed the presence of Lucretius at line 335, where the words *atrae Formidinis ora* are drawn directly from the fourth book of *De Rerum Natura*. As Turnus metamorphosizes from instiller of terror to terrified when death approaches, Lucretius is still present in Virgil's mind to help detail the symptoms.

His rhetoric might also have helped stimulate Virgil's imagination to create one of the psychological masterstrokes of his poem. In the Lucretius passage we join with our teacher in examining the symptoms of fear, in learning through autopsy what those symptoms mean (*videmus*, *videmus*). In Virgil, by brilliant contrast, we join with the victim in undergoing the same experiences (*videmur*, *succidimus*). From clinical outsiders, learning from a master in *De Rerum Natura*, we ourselves have evolved, through Virgil's magic, into participants in enduring the actuality of suffering.

Such a use of the first person in narrative is unique in the poem. It achieves the effect of having us become Turnus. The immortalizing poet would seem to intervene directly in the cases of Nisus and Euryalus and of Lausus,[146] all of whom are apostrophized, and the narrator's address to Pallas at 10. 507 comes at a moment of particular poignancy. In book 4, as we have seen, the narrator apostrophizes Dido as she watches Aeneas depart with the result that we are urged to understand the circumstances of her ordeal from close at hand. But there is no parallel for Virgil employing his rhetorical skills to effectuate our actually becoming one with a character in the story. That he chooses Turnus instead of Aeneas as the object for this display of virtuosity, that he chooses suffering victim rather than wrathful killer, is not lost on his readers.

Turnus is the primary locus of emotionality throughout book 12. At the start we watch the response to his predicament on the part of the old king Latinus, of Lavinia with her famous blush, of Amata, the "beloved," as her name suggests, whose devotion to her prospective son-in-law, we recall, was already described to us in book 7 as "an astonishing love" (*miro amore*).[147] She is soon to die (*moritura*, 55), a state denied to the goddess Juturna, the sister whose support of, and dependency upon, her doomed sibling are central to some of the poem's most moving final moments. And we have seen how, through the poem's last long simile, we, narrator and readers alike, not only identify with but suffer together with the enfeebled, torpid hero.

Our sympathies are further aroused by the careful analogies Virgil's allusiveness draws between the stricken warrior and figures such as Hector, Dido, and an earlier, suffering Aeneas. We have examined closely the brief vignettes in book 10 where Aeneas seizes eight victims for subsequent sacrifice and then kills suppliant after suppliant. The last three hundred and fifty lines of book 12 are a broadly expansive version of both topics. Turnus is both Aeneas's final suppliant and his final human sacrifice. It is for both reasons, but primarily as a victim, that he elicits the enormous empathy of poet and therefore reader alike.

There is also a way in which Virgil adds the voice of ethical authority to the sympathy that he arouses for Turnus. To see this we must turn back to the epic's ultimate scene in heaven that occurs just before the concluding duel commences. The episode consists of a dialogue between Jupiter and Juno in which we take final note of the enormous resentment (*tantus dolor*, 801), the huge floods of wrath (*irarum tantos fluctus*, 831), and the fury (*furorem*, 832) that since the beginning of the epic have characterized the goddess's emotional response to Aeneas and to his fellow Trojans. Jupiter orders her to press her vendetta no further. The king of the gods and warden of fate pronounces that the newcomers and the aboriginal Latins, once the war is over, will merge and live at peace. Juno rejoices and nods approval.

But Virgil seldom leaves matters with such a straightforward outcome. One complication here resides in the phraseology that the husband uses as he commands his wife to abandon her violent ways: "I forbid you to essay [your present course of action] any further" ('...*ulterius temptare veto*,' 806). Virgil would have us remember Jupiter's words in the final language he gives Turnus, now wounded suppliant, asking his victor for forbearance as Aeneas contemplates his next course of action. We will discuss the moment in detail later. Let us examine here only the humbled hero's last words (12. 936–38):

> '...vicisti et victum tendere palmas
> Ausonii videre; tua est Lavinia coniunx,
> ulterius ne tende odiis.'

"You have conquered, and the Ausonii have seen me, conquered, stretch forth my hands. Lavinia is your wife. Do not continue any further in your stretches of hatred."

The words of Jupiter and Turnus conspire. *Tempto* and *tendo* are cognate verbs with overlapping meanings, here suggesting aims that should come to a halt. Both phrases are negative commands. Both climactically bring speeches to an end with an order. Together they contain the only two examples of *ulterius* in the Virgilian corpus. They further stand out here as opening their respective hexameters as well as forming the conclusion of speeches that come at crucial moments for the interpretation of the poem's ethical values.

The parallel can be looked at both as a generality and for the meaning of its particulars. In drawing an equation between Jupiter and Turnus, Virgil would have us see the stricken hero in his moment of prayer as the terrestrial, mortal counterpart of the omnipotent ruler of heaven. He takes on, even in his physical debilitation but perhaps also because of it, the role of earthly patriarch. Virgil has carefully had Turnus, in lines immediately preceding those quoted above, remind Aeneas of "Anchises his begetter" (*Anchises genitor*, 934). It is Anchises who, as we have seen in book 6, has entreated his son to be a model for future Romans while he himself prepares to cope with the war to come (853):

> 'parcere subiectis et debellare superbos.'

"...to spare the humbled and war down the haughty."

The restraint that Jupiter asks of his wife in heaven Turnus, the suppliant, now pleads for on earth from his conqueror. It is a similar holding back that Anchises had preached to Aeneas in the underworld. So Virgil accords to Turnus's final words great prestige, thereby granting him a share in the authority of the patriarch of the gods in heaven and of Aeneas's father on earth, both asking for moderation and for thought before action, but also for restraint in the behavior of their interlocutor.

Let us look in particular at the word *odiis*. As commentators agree, the plural of *odium* means repeated acts of hatred and hostility. Since Cicero defines *odium* as "long-standing anger" (*ira inveterata*),[148] anger that has become habitual, *odia* implies a continuity of wrath expressed over a length of time. Though he offers no explanation, Turnus, and we through him, could well see this hatred as manifested in the spate of killings after the death of Pallas of which Turnus himself will soon be the last example, or in the unprovoked burning of Latinus's city and its concomitant suffering.[149]

When we think of repeated manifestations of *odium*, and its companion *ira*, throughout the *Aeneid*, Virgil would have us center our thoughts primarily on Juno. At 1. 668, Venus can speak to Cupid of the "hatreds of bitter Juno" (*odiis Iunonis acerbae*) against his brother, and at 5. 781 she begins an address to Neptune with mention of "Juno's heavy wrath" (*Iunonis gravis ira*) and pursues her theme by telling of the continuum of the elemental hatred (*odiis*, 786) that she, Juno, vents against Troy and Trojans. At 7. 298, Juno herself can call attention to her hatreds (*odiis*), which will soon be evinced in hatreds that the fury Allecto is preparing to stir up in the Latin world (*odiis*, 336). And as we have already seen, the anger of Juno is mentioned three times in the first twenty-five lines of the poem so as to stay with the reader throughout its course.

When Jupiter lectures Juno at line 805, it is his rational, moderating side that is in the ascendant, not his vengeful aspect exhibited by the Fury he sends down like a whirlwind to enfeeble Turnus, or its reappearance in Aeneas's spear that "flies like a black whirlwind" (*volat atri turbinis instar*, 923) and "carries dread doom" (*exitium dirum ferens*, 924).[150] The same must be said for his earthly complement, Turnus, as he implores Aeneas to give him his life.[151] That Aeneas hesitates means that at least for a moment he ponders the possibility of sparing his suppliant, which is to say of renouncing the *odia* that Turnus perceives in his previous actions. Can Turnus play Jupiter to Aeneas's Juno and persuade him, as Aeneas's father would have urged, to spare the suppliant now that his pride has been humbled?[152]

The answer, we soon learn, is negative. After seeing the sword belt of Pallas on Turnus's shoulder, the spirit of revenge sweeps over Aeneas. Driven by the memory of his "savage resentment" (*saevi doloris*, 945) at the death of his handsome protégé, he kills, "set aflame by furies and terrifying in his anger" (*furiis accensus et ira / terribilis*, 946–47). Virgil, as has long been noted, associates this lexicon of emotionality from the start of the poem with Juno angrily pursuing her vendetta against Aeneas and his fellow exiles. We have earlier traced its recurrences, culminating in the goddess's renunciation of her anger to Jupiter before the final scene commences. But Aeneas's emotionality upon seeing Pallas's baldric is stronger than any feelings of clemency that Turnus-Jupiter-Anchises might suggest and that for a moment seem in fact to restrain Aeneas from any further physical action against his suppliant foe. The intensities of Juno that Virgil detailed at the epic's start now take on their own new individuality in his hero who, unlike the goddess at the epic's start, has the will and power to take the life of his foe that flees beneath the shades. And, as we have seen, Virgil has been at pains to contrast this madness with the authority that the poet lends the hero's defeated foe as the epic draws to a close.

In the next chapter we conclude by examining some further details in the poem's ending itself.

CHAPTER 6

The Ending

ACHILLES: Look, Hector, how the sun begins to set;
How ugly night comes breathing at his heels.
Even with the vail and dark'ning of the sun,
To close the day up, Hector's life is done.
HECTOR: I am unarmed; forgo this vantage, Greek.
ACHILLES: Strike, fellows, strike! This is the man I seek.
[*Hector falls.*]
So, Ilion, fall thou next! Now, Troy, sink down!
Here lies thy heart, thy sinews, and thy bone.

Shakespeare, *Troilus amd Cressida*, Act V, Scene 8

I N CONCLUSION, let us turn to the epic's final thirty lines.[153] Aeneas brandishes and hurls his spear that flies toward Turnus like rocks from a catapult, like the roar of lightening bolts, or a black whirlwind. It pierces the thigh of its victim, who falls to the ground, his knee doubled under him (930–38):

> ille humilis supplex oculos dextramque precantem
> protendens 'equidem merui nec deprecor' inquit;
> 'utere sorte tua. miseri te si qua parentis
> tangere cura potest, oro (fuit et tibi talis
> Anchises genitor) Dauni miserere senectae
> et me, seu corpus spoliatum lumine mavis,
> redde meis. vicisti et victum tendere palmas
> Ausonii videre; tua est Lavinia coniunx
> ulterius ne tende odiis.'

He, a suppliant, with eyes humbled and stretching forth his right hand in prayer says "Indeed I have deserved [my fate] nor do I pray it away. Use your chance. If any care of a sad parent can touch you, I pray you, pity the old age of Daunus (Anchises was also such a father to you) and return me or, if you prefer, my body bereft of light to my people. You have conquered and the Ausonians have seen me, conquered, stretch forth my hands. Lavinia is your wife. Do not press further in your hatred."

In his final words the suppliant hero admits the justice of his humiliation by Aeneas, gives up any claim to Lavinia, and asks for an end to hatred. He offers his victor a chance to spare him by entreating that either he or his body be returned to his kin. In the course of pleading for pity not for himself, be it noted, but for his father, Daunus, he reminds his conqueror of the latter's own father, Anchises, whom Aeneas and the readers of his epic have last seen in the extraordinary conclusion to the sixth book. There, we recall, father reminded son, addressed as *Romane*, that it was the duty of the empowered Roman warrior to abase the prideful but also to practice forbearance on those brought low.

Aeneas hesitates. This is the last and most crucial of such pauses that in Virgil's text take us from Dido, lingering before departure on her fateful day of hunting, from the golden bough hesitating before Aeneas plucks it and initiates the history of Rome, to Vulcan pausing before crafting that same history on Aeneas's shield to give it further permanence, finally to this moment where the patriarchal dictum is put to its climactic test.[154] But upon seeing on Turnus's shoulder the baldric of Pallas that Turnus had torn from the youth's body after slaying him, Aeneas grows furious and kills (945–52):

> ille, oculis postquam saevi monimenta doloris
> exuviasque hausit, furiis accensus et ira
> terribilis: 'tune hinc spoliis indute meorum
> eripiare mihi? Pallas te hoc vulnere, Pallas
> immolat et poenam scelerato ex sanguine sumit.'
> hoc dicens ferrum adverso sub pectore condit
> fervidus; ast illi solvuntur frigore membra
> vitaque cum gemitu fugit indignata sub umbras.

After he had drunk in with his eyes the memorials of his savage grief and the spoils, inflamed by furies and frightening in his anger: "Are you, clothed in the spoils of what belongs to me, to be snatched from me? Pallas, Pallas sacrifices you with this wound and exacts punishment from your criminal blood." Saying this, ablaze with anger he buries his sword beneath the chest of his enemy. [Turnus's] limbs grow slack from chill, and with a groan his life flees, resentful, under the shades.

There is a relentless negativity to this conclusion that the poet leaves unresolved. He presents us with nothing parallel to the cathartic events that bring Virgil's primary model, Homer's *Iliad*, to an end — no funeral games for Patroclus, no ransoming of Hector's body, nothing akin to the powerful concluding lamentations for the Trojan prince. The poet offers us no relief from Aeneas's all-consuming fury, no transcendence into a different emotional or intellectual sphere. Neither through the words of his hero nor within the narration does Virgil come to the defense of his violent action. He gives us no sense that Aeneas kills either to secure his own heroic stature as his poem concludes or to rid the world of negative opposition to his immediate fate or to more distant Roman accomplishments.[155]

On the contrary, according to the poet, Aeneas's enraged killing stems from remembrance of his savage, though natural, grief at the death of Pallas and of its concomitant resentment. His action could be said to bring to a close a vendetta on behalf of Evander by his serving in the place of an aged father and slaying his son's slayer. If so, Virgil offers us no relieving or exonerating evidence. Instead he shows his hero going directly against his own father's command to spare the humbled and instead manifesting a very human, if disconcerting, response to the sight of the killer of his protégé now at his mercy.

Though they may be troubling to the reader, the narrator's feelings seem clear. The poem itself provides an ethical frame in which we expect Aeneas to operate and against which his final action must be judged. Time and again throughout its course the epic offers evidence against the moral appropriateness of the hero's last deed. We have already surveyed several instances of this commentary in detail. Let us begin, however, by recapitulation. We will follow the path of the narration and watch how fraught these final lines are with previous evidence that comments on the morality of Aeneas's concluding act. As in our earlier practice, Virgil's own language will serve as our primary guide.

We end the epic with Aeneas "inflamed by furies and frightening in his anger" (*furiis accensus et ira / terribilis*) as a result of being reminded of his "savage grief" (*saevi doloris*) at the death of Pallas. We begin the poem with a triple reference to the *ira* of Juno.[156] This wrath is likewise connected with grief and resentment. At line 9 the queen of the gods is *dolens*, and at 25 we learn further of her *saevi dolores*. Her anger is directed against Aeneas and the Trojans and is based on sexual jealousy because of the judgment of Trojan Paris, who had favored Venus over her, and because of the preferment granted Trojan Ganymede by Jupiter. We will turn shortly to the erotic element present in Aeneas's final burst of anger. Suffice it to say here that Virgil thus establishes a careful cycle between the beginning and the conclusion of his epic, centered among other specific ways on anger, which itself contains a strong passional component.

Both Juno at the start and Aeneas at the conclusion, as now in power he becomes his own form of wrathful Juno, are carrying out a destructive vendetta of vengeance. Juno fails in her attempt to obliterate the remnants of Troy while Aeneas-Juno by contrast succeeds in slaying the killer of Pallas. But both behave inordinately in their anger, especially through its ruinous physical manifestations that are far out of scale by comparison to its causes: Juno bent on annihilation by means of the violent storm with which the epic opens, Aeneas first through his rampage in book 10 and then through the enraged killing of a suppliant with which the poem ends.

Another patent cycle complements the repetition of the vocabulary of emotion between beginning and end, namely the reflection and elaboration of the epic's opening words, *Arma virumque*, in the narrative of its finale. Virgil forewarns us at the poem's start that we will be attending to the relationship between arms and a man but it is only in its concluding lines that we watch the crucial demonstration of the symbiosis between Aeneas, his weaponry, and its use. We readers join the story's spectators as Virgil has us watch closely the actions of the hero, first hurling the spear that wounds Turnus, then driving the fatal sword into his heart.

Another piece of armor figures pivotally as well in the finale, the sword belt of Pallas. Between Aeneas's spear toss and sword thrust comes the moment of pause where we wait to see whether the words of victim will affect the actions of victor. But sight of Pallas's baldric not only breaks the respite but also incites him to kill. The last conjunction of man and his weapons proves as passionate as it is deadly.

Parallels between beginning and end help outline some major differences between these two scenes. The poet assists us in putting this evolution in place. We can start by calling attention again to how Virgil describes Aeneas when he is first named (1. 91):

> extemplo Aeneae solvuntur frigore membra...

> suddenly the limbs of Aeneas grow slack from cold...

The hero in book 1, whose limbs grow numb in the face of Juno's death-threatening tempest, is at the conclusion replaced by Turnus, his victim —

> ...ast illi solvuntur frigore membra...

> but his limbs grow slack from cold —

as the goddess's anger and its brutal manifestation become now incorporated in the victorious hero bent on retaliation. And on a larger scale the fear that the Trojans experience through a good deal of book 1 is now transferred to Turnus himself, prey to both Fury and furious hero.[157]

As the storm ends in book 1, Neptune, calmer of tempests, is compared in the epic's first simile to a man who assuages with words a rebellious mob to which "fury supplies weapons" (*furor arma ministrat*, 150). Virgil's words suggest a comparison between the god "weighty with piety" (*pi-*

etate gravem, 151) and Aeneas, whom the narrator near the start styled "outstanding for piety" (*insignem pietate*, 10). It is a different hero whom we meet at the end. The implicitly divine calmer of *furor* becomes himself the embodiment of fury in operation. And he who was likened to someone utilizing words to forestall further physical violence now fails to attend to his suppliant opponent's prayerful speech, which has the potential to propose that clemency might be in order toward his defeated foe.

When Aeneas at the end exchanges places with the Juno whom we first meet, Virgil offers us no calming Neptune figure to put a stop to unnecessary violence. Prideful Turnus, after all, to rephrase Anchises's precept, has been roundly, publicly vanquished and restraint from further use of force is in order. But we have come a far cry from the selfless, long-suffering Aeneas of books 1 to 4, bearing his father on his shoulders away from the flames of Troy, withstanding the turmoil stirred by Juno's insatiable enmity, and putting the destiny of Rome ahead of personal feeling in his abandonment of Dido. As the sufferer metamorphoses into the inflictor of suffering, Virgil has Aeneas shunt aside the new ethical framework proposed by his father for the behavior of a victorious hero toward his foe, a framework that would distinguish the *Aeneid* from its great Homeric model. Instead of having his hero serve as a humane exemplar for Rome of the self-control and moderation in victory that Anchises's words project, of a collective responsibility to an ethic of forbearance, Virgil leaves him a prey to individualistic emotionality, which ignites an Achillean anger insistent on the need for retribution.

Let us now turn to an event earlier in the epic's chronology but later in its narrative, Aeneas's abortive attempt to kill Helen, which he describes to the listening Dido.[158] This is the first instance in the epic of Aeneas in fury and Virgil is at pains to connect the event in the reader's mind with the equally vindictive rage of the hero at the epic's end.

We first hear of Aeneas's fury at line 588 when he speaks to Dido of being carried away "by a frenzied mind" (*furiata mente*) as he contemplated the killing of Helen, whom he has discovered seeking asylum at the threshold of Troy's temple of Vesta. His state of mind is confirmed by Venus, who first grabs him by her right hand and holds him back from any act of physical reprisal against the woman whom he earlier called the common Fury of both Troy and her own fatherland. His mother's words begin (594–95):

> 'nate, quis indomitas tantus dolor excitat iras?
> quid furis? aut quonam nostri tibi cura recessit?'

"My son, what huge resentment stirs your ungovernable wrath? Why are you raging? Or whither has your care for us vanished?"

Virgil co-opts the language of parent voicing concern with her offspring's potential violence and its immorality into his own narrative of Aeneas's motivation as his epic ends (945–47):

> ille, oculis postquam saevi monumenta doloris
> exuviasque hausit, furiis accensus et ira
> terribilis:...

As we said, vengeance is operative in both situations. In the first instance it is posited against Helen for the ruin of Troy, and in the second against Turnus for the death of Pallas. In book 2 an appearance of Venus physically prohibits such an inappropriate display of a hero's force. At the end, Virgil's words press the reader to remember that Aeneas is now in a parallel situation to that in which he found himself when confronting Helen.

But just as Turnus's mention of Anchises fails to remind his son of his duty according to his father's commanding rhetoric to spare suppliants, so before the final killing no epiphany of his mother takes place, as in the case of his confrontation with Helen, to chide her son and to prevent him from putting his fury into destructive action against Turnus. In both instances the reader remembers words that the hero should recall but does not, words stemming from both parents that should properly direct his actions at the epic's conclusion but fail to do so.

One further allusion corroborates the link between the episode in book 2 and the ending. Aeneas's last words to Turnus before the fatal sword thrust consist of an emotional appeal to the dead Pallas (948–49):

> '...Pallas te hoc vulnere, Pallas
> immolat et poenam scelerato ex sanguine sumit.'

"Pallas, Pallas sacrifices you with this wound and exacts punishment from your criminal blood."

As he readies himself to kill, Aeneas remembers the death of Pallas and in his final words in the poem sees himself as the young hero's surrogate as he prepares to slay his slayer.

Virgil however would have his reader recall Aeneas's own description to Dido of how emotion overcame him on catching sight of Helen in Vesta's shadow (2. 575–76):

'...subit ira cadentem
ulcisci patriam et sceleratas sumere poenas.'

"...anger overcomes me to avenge my falling fatherland and to exact punishment for her crimes."

These are the only two instances in the poem where Virgil uses forms of *sceleratus*, *sumo*, and *poena* together,[159] and the impressive assemblage gains further force because of the presence of *ira* (2. 575; 12. 946) as part of the concatenation. Both moments center on the hero's need and desire for revenge.[160] Both find him driven by anger. In the first instance his mother's epiphany puts a stop to violent action. (For Aeneas actually to kill a woman would be unthinkable.) In the second situation, Virgil allows no such intervention either from without or from Aeneas's own memory and sensibility.

Virgil adds to his point by having the allusions to the second book at the poem's conclusion work in reverse. At the end of the poem we are first reminded of Venus's prohibition against anger, then of Aeneas's inner need for punitive redress, which initiates his tale of seeing Helen. The resulting chiasmus is the poet's further way of eliminating the goddess's calming speech, now by replacing it for the reader with a reminder of the hero's thwarted desire for retaliation against "Troy's Fury." This prompting on Virgil's part reinforces the vividness of the vengeful killing that immediately follows as the epic concludes.

Let us now turn for a final time to the figure of Dido. We have talked earlier about how the language associated with Dido's death permeates the final book, especially when Virgil is dealing with the suicide of Amata and the forced departure from the action of Turnus's supportive sister Juturna. Let us also recall the extraordinary opening simile where Turnus is compared to a wounded lion (12. 4–6):

...Poenorum qualis in arvis
saucius ille gravi venantum vulnere pectus
tum demum movet arma leo, ...

We earlier mentioned how the particular force of this analogy stems in part from the fact that warriors are regularly compared to lions as they pursue their victims, or are pursued, in the heat of battle, but that here by contrast we enter the emotional, not the physical, life of the poem's hero. We also noted that he draws directly on the opening lines of book 4 for the words that he chooses (4. 1–2):

At regina gravi iamdudum saucia cura
vulnus alit venis et caeco carpitur igni.

But the queen, now long stricken by grievous distress, nourished the
wound from her veins and is seized by hidden fire.

Since the language of Dido as used in connection with several of its major
characters permeates the epic's final book, it is appropriate for several
reasons that Turnus be understood as one of the most salient reincar-
nations of the doomed queen as the epic runs its course. As also in the
case of Dido, his emotional wounding at the start of the book suffers
metamorphosis into the fatal sword thrust that kills him at the end. If we
follow out the nuances of the simile, his psychic hurt stems from one of
a troop of hunters (*venantum*, 12. 5) who is also a robber (*latronis*, 7). This
is to say that, at least in his eyes, Aeneas is the predator bent on stealing
Lavinia from him. (We remember that in the first simile of book 4 Aeneas
is a shepherd wounding Dido as deer and at 12. 751 he is a *venator canis*,
a hunter-hound.)

And as in the history of Dido, emotional but figurative injury at the
start leads to the reality of physical death at the end. The major difference between the two episodes is of course that the Carthaginian queen's
decease is of her own making. Aeneas is only vicariously present as the
owner of the sword by which she commits suicide. In book 12, by contrast, Aeneas is the actual bringer of doom to his enemy. From one point
of view it could even be said that he kills the embodiment of his former
lover.

But Virgil's words again have still more to tell us and to have us ponder. Aeneas kills Turnus-Dido, but he also incarnates her as well. As she
utters her last speech of prayer to Aeneas, she styles herself as "set afire
by furies" (*furiis incensa*, 4. 376) and shortly later the narrator confirms
her situation as a moment "when, overwhelmed by grief, she absorbed
the furies and decided on death..." (*ubi concepit furias evicta dolore / decre-
vitque mori...*, 4. 474–75). Aeneas, too, as he kills, we remember, is *furiis
accensus*, the passive victim of inner furies with a remembrance of his
own "savage grief" (*saevi doloris*).[161]

So, as we look at the end of the *Aeneid* through the prism of the emotional world that Virgil creates for Dido and which stays with us throughout the epic, Aeneas both becomes her and kills her as he slays Turnus,
but with one major difference. Dido is the passive victim of furies who
opts for self-slaughter. Aeneas is equally a prey to madness but turns its
violent manifestation onto his suppliant opponent.

We move now to book 10 and to the adventures of Pallas and to his death, which motivates Aeneas to kill at the end. Let us first turn to Pallas himself. Only by recapitulating Virgil's depiction of the youth in book 8 and of his attachment to Aeneas can we begin to fathom reasons for the feverishness of the hero's response to his killing in book 10 and to its remembrance in book 12.

Virgil would have us both hear tell of and watch the beauty of the young prince. His father Evander speaks of him, preparing to depart for battle, in erotic terms as "my only and late delight" (*mea sola et sera voluptas*, 8. 581) and shortly later Virgil compares him to the Morning Star (590):

> ...quem Venus ante alios astrorum diligit ignis.

> ...whom Venus loves ahead of the other fiery stars.[162]

But we are made to sense the androgynous beauty of Pallas most pointedly when we join in watching Aeneas gaze at his lifeless corpse (11. 39–40):

> ipse caput nivei fultum Pallantis et ora
> ut vidit levique patens in pectore vulnus...

> When he himself saw the pillowed head and face of snow-white Pallas and the gaping wound on his smooth breast...

The narrator further emphasizes the femininity of his charm shortly later by comparing him to a violet or hyacinth.[163]

Finally, in conjunction with Pallas's funeral, Virgil offers his reader a series of associations with Dido. The first line of book 11 is an exact repetition of line 129 of book 4 as Dido and Aeneas embark on their fateful hunt, and the Carthaginian queen is directly mentioned at line 74 as the weaver of two pieces of cloth, one of which Aeneas uses to wrap the body of the dead youth.[164]

Dido also figures at another crucial moment, the only occasion where Virgil allows us to see Aeneas and Pallas together. The two are journeying from Pallanteum to enter the battle that will soon be fatal to the young hero. Aeneas ponders the events of the war (10. 160–62):

> ...Pallasque sinistro
> adfixus lateri iam quaerit sidera, opacae
> noctis iter, iam quae passus terraque marique.

...and Pallas, pinioned to his left side,[165] inquires now about the stars, the course of the dark night, now of what he suffered on land and sea.

We are on a boat venturing down the Tiber, but Virgil's words also locate us with Dido at the conclusion of the epic's first book as she listens first to Iopas sing about the ways of the heavens and then to Aeneas detail his adventures, beginning with Troy's demise and leading to his arrival at Carthage. And it is the repetition of the same history, we are told near the start of book 4, that further confirms the Carthaginian queen's infatuation with her handsome visitor.[166]

The erotic suggestiveness via a connection between Pallas and Dido is maintained in the extraordinary metaphor *adfixus lateri*. We noted earlier that the only exact linguistic parallel elsewhere in the epic occurs at 9. 536, where Turnus is attacking a tower outside the Trojan ramparts (535–37):

> princeps ardentem coniecit lampada Turnus
> et flammam adfixit lateri, quae plurima vento
> corripuit tabulas et postibus haesit adesis.

Turnus in the forefront hurled a blazing torch and fastened the flame to its side. Swollen by the wind, it seized the planks and clung to the beams it had eaten through.

Another close parallel occurs later in the book as a fatal arrow "lodges deep in a warrior's left side" (*sagitta /...laevo infixa est alte lateri...*).[167] So as we change from literal to figurative language, from battle scenes where fire and arrows are on display as weapons to Pallas clinging to Aeneas's left side, we take with us through metaphor the same erotic language, as we have seen, with which book 4 opens:

> At regina gravi iamdudum saucia cura
> vulnus alit venis et caeco carpitur igni.

Pallas is to Aeneas as Aeneas is to Dido. He is at once a firebrand, stuck to Aeneas's side, that could set emotion afire, or an arrow that equally causes an inner wound.

We find confirmation for Virgil's suggestiveness in a poem of the elegist Tibullus where the poet's speaker is inveighing against riches and the rich lover who can buy the affections that he desires. By contrast:

pauper erit praesto tibi semper; pauper adibit
primus et in tenero fixus erit latere.[168]

The poor man will always be at hand for you. The poor man will come
to you first and will cling to your tender side.

Though the sexes are reversed, the metaphor for a lover's constancy and
attachment as something pierced into the beloved's side remains similar. The difference lies chiefly in the fact that Virgil elaborates for us by
illustration elsewhere exactly what metaphoric forms this emotional
earnestness might take, earnestness with a potentially destructive cast.
In the case of Dido, the fire and the wound caused by Aeneas lead only
to her self-annihilation at the end of book 4. In the case of Aeneas, the
spiritual equivalent of the torch or arrow that Virgil uses elsewhere to
describe palpable destructiveness is, first, the emotional bond that Virgil's metaphors ask us to sense between hero and protégé. But when that
attachment is severed as it is here through Turnus's slaughter of Pallas in
battle, then its potentially ruinous character as metaphor takes tangible
form in Aeneas's vengeful reaction, in the rage that takes the life of the
person who had deprived him of his prized possession.

Virgil's language again comes to our aid in making the transition from
this initiatory moment in book 10, as hero and companion boat down the
river, to the emotion-ridden killing of Turnus, which is to say, from metaphor to the realization of the figuration's deadly potential at the end.
We have earlier examined in detail the spate of violent mayhem on which
Aeneas embarks later in the book after learning of Pallas's death. One
theme stands out, we noted, in Virgil's description of Aeneas's savagery,
namely, the offering of human sacrifice to the shades as an essential part
of his retaliation. In this case, literal and figurative work together. Aeneas begins his rampage by taking eight victims so that he can "drench
the flames of the pyre with blood of the captives" (*captivo...rogi perfundat
sanguine flammas*, 10. 520), and we hear of them again when they form
part of Pallas's funeral cortege as Aeneas "is about to sprinkle the flames
with blood of the slaughtered" (*caeso sparsurus sanguine flammas*, 11. 82).

On the first occasion the notion that the human victims are actually
sacrificial is reinforced by Virgil's use of the verb *immolare* to characterize
Aeneas's action: they are chosen so that he can "render oblation to the
shades" (*inferias...immolet umbris*, 10. 519). Virgil soon repeats the verb
as Aeneas slays the priest Haemonides, whom the hero stands over and
kills specifically as sacrifice (*immolat*, 541) — a particularly ironic example
of the sacrificer sacrificed so that human victim serves in the place of

animal. Virgil's third and last use of the verb occurs at 12. 949 where, as we have seen, Virgil puts it into the mouth of Aeneas himself to characterize his killing of Turnus as the offering of a sacrificial victim (*immolat*, 12. 949).

The emotional connection that Virgil suggests in book 10 between Aeneas and Pallas and that makes itself vividly apparent in the savage form his murderous rage takes after the youth's death thus manifests itself dramatically again at the epic's end. It is stirred by the sight of Pallas's baldric on Turnus, which reminds him of his wild grief at the youth's death. By having us also in our turn think back to Aeneas's rage in book 10 and in particular by his use of *immolare*, twice prominent in the earlier episode, for one final time, Virgil closely links the two episodes for his readers. With the help of book 10 we can then see the end of the poem as the continuation of Aeneas's extravagant display of emotionality at Pallas's death. His fury there is reignited by the sight of Pallas's baldric, and his wrathful killing of the suppliant Turnus, against his father's command, becomes the last in the series of human sacrifices that Aeneas feels the need to perform, certainly to pay tribute to Pallas and to avenge his death, but apparently also to compensate himself in an especially horrifying way for the gravity of his own personal loss and perhaps even guilt.

We have seen how earlier events in book 12 itself can assist in the interpretation of its conclusion, and especially how the figure of Dido in various poetic metamorphoses runs through the book from beginning to end. But there is a moment not far from the conclusion that can help explain one of the more startling expressions in Aeneas's final words to Turnus:

> 'tune hinc spoliis indute meorum
> eripiare mihi?'

"Are you, clothed in the spoils of what belongs to me, to be snatched from me?"

The word *meorum* is usually translated with a phrase like "of one of my people"[169] or "of one of mine" with no explanation of where "one" comes from or why Pallas, son of Evander, should be an example of Aeneas's particular Trojan retinue. That it should have the full force of "what belongs to me," an announcement of possessiveness whose force is strengthened by the subsequent *mihi*, is corroborated by Juturna's emotional words to her brother shortly before, at 882–83, as she prepares to depart from

Turnus's side at the command of Jupiter. Were she not immortal, she cries, she would suffer death to follow him into the Underworld (882–83):

> '...aut quicquam mihi dulce meorum
> te sine, frater, erit?'

> "...or will anything of what is mine be sweet to me, brother, without you?"

The proximity of *meorum* and *mihi* in both passages emphasizes the deep emotionality of each situation and indeed their similarities. Juturna's loss of Turnus is parallel to Aeneas's deprivation of Pallas. Yet a difference remains. In the case of Juturna, there is no singular referent revealed to us about what *meorum* might mean. For Aeneas, the reader knows the particular significance of *meorum*. It is Pallas who "belongs" to Aeneas and whose loss drives him not to leave the scene of battling as in the case of Juturna, but to kill the person who deprived him of what he considered his. Virgil's language strongly argues for the intimacy between the two scenes.[170]

I have mentioned before the importance of possessiveness as the epic draws to a close. Here it becomes paramount. As he himself puts it, Pallas belongs to Aeneas. For him to practice any form of restraint at this climactic moment would be to cede this most emotional of possessions to Turnus by granting him his life without avenging the loss of Pallas. For Aeneas to reclaim Pallas, he cannot allow Turnus to be "snatched away" alive. The killing of Turnus wearing Pallas's sword belt, the sudden epiphanic appearance of which initiates Aeneas's decisive display of rage, brings back under Aeneas's deadly sway both the killer and the killed. No forbearance, no stoic submission to patriarchal command against such violence, is possible when this double need for dominion governs the hero's actions during his paroxysm of pain and hatred. To spare, to throw away the weapons of vengeance — here I paraphrase Anchises again — would be to abandon the personal for the impersonal. It would replace the all-too-available propensity for physical reprisal for hurt inflicted with a spiritual dogma that dispenses with vendetta and with the use of mortal force against a vanquished suppliant. It does so in favor of a clemency that not only spares but presumably initiates the healing of rifts and a return to humane values for both parties.

I have focused particular attention on the poem's conclusion for multiple reasons. First, the fact that Virgil asks us to dwell in our memories on earlier passages from throughout his masterpiece to help us appreciate some of the force of its conclusion eliminates any doubt about the importance of seeing the ending as superbly conceived and definitive. We read the poem as a cycle leading from Juno's storm of elemental jealousy and anger to Aeneas's final convulsion from parallel emotions, from the founding of Rome that we hear of at the epic's start (*conderet*, 1. 5) to the burial of Aeneas's sword in the chest of his enemy (*condit*, 12. 950). But we also draw on the worlds of Helen and Venus, of Dido and Anchises, of Evander, Pallas, Turnus and others, to help explain some of Virgil's rich meanings.

The unsaid also plays a major part in how we proceed with the work of interpretation. Virgil does not end the poem, as we might expect of a great epic performance, with the hero in glory. Far from it. And, as I have said before, the poet offers us nothing of Homer's palliatives after the death of Patroclus — funeral games for Achilles's comrade, the ransom by Priam of the body of Hector, and the triple lamentations for him that bring the *Iliad* to such an enormously moving conclusion.

But the most striking omission is that of Rome itself. Virgil has after all presented his poem not only as the saga of Aeneas surmounting the difficulties of transferring Troy to Pallanteum but also as a learning experience for the reader. We move from Jupiter's glowing announcement of future Roman glory in book 1 to the brilliant parade of heroes to come presided over by Anchises in book 6, to the shield Vulcan manufactures in book 8, whose culminating scene shows Augustus in triumph on the steps of his gleaming new Temple to Apollo. And in the final book we find Jupiter allaying Juno's worries near the epic's end by pointing to Roman grandeur in time to come.

Rome is therefore always in the poem's background just as the world of Italy, the richly varied land of peoples and places that fostered Roman ambitions, remains ever present at least for the last seven books before the reader's imagination. But the ending urges our thoughts in a different direction. Anchises addresses his son in the underworld as *Romane*, as the epitome of Roman heroes yet to be born. And often during the course of the poem we have watched the nobility of leadership that he displays. A prominent example would be the moment earlier in the final book where a helmetless Aeneas, given his epithet *pius* for the last time in the poem, asks his army to explain the sudden outburst of dissension (*discordia*, 12. 313), and pleads that they restrain their anger (*iras*, 314). But it is not on Aeneas as incipient Roman, as the initiatory model for Rome's particular form or forms of heroism, that Virgil would have us concentrate at his epic's climax. There is no self-effacement in victory, no abstract curbing of emotion against the prideful now laid low, no general pronouncement of Roman cultural and political accomplishments to come now that the demons of opposition have been removed.[171]

No final reluctance, not to say generosity, here calls a halt to killing so as to forestall further mutual hatred. There is no gesture toward reconciliation nor even any concessions in its direction. Rather, Virgil would have us concentrate on Aeneas the individual human being betraying profoundly felt human emotions and yielding, here at least, to their negative force.[172] Nor is there on display now any of the hero's wonted piety in which to take pride. As we have seen, Aeneas has ignored the moderating words of both his parents. And though earlier in the final book he asks for the bridling of anger on the part of his soldiery, at its conclusion wrath rules his own actions. Aeneas remains a vengeful Achilles, but an Achilles without the latter's redeeming pity for Priam, a pity that Turnus asks him to show toward his father Daunus but to which Aeneas fails to respond.[173]

Virgil thus leaves us to study this extraordinary concluding amalgam of passion and power with a deepened understanding of the humanness of Aeneas, and perhaps of all heroes. He may have meant us to see this honest presentation rather than some gilded paean of praise for emperor and empire as his greatest gift to Rome and Augustus, to literature, and so on to us, for certainly those are the final thoughts that he bequeaths to his readers.[174]

The ancient *vitae* report that on his deathbed Virgil wished that the manuscript of the *Aeneid* be burned so that no trace of his epic would remain for posterity. If I were to hazard a guess as to why such might have been the poet's desire, it would not stem from the fact that in the end he was riddled with doubts about any hypothetical eulogy of empire that he had been expected to deliver, a eulogy that might be discerned in the adventures of his hero, or in his vignettes of Augustus's golden time to come. Rather, I would suggest, and I'm not the first to do so, that his wish to destroy his final masterpiece would more likely arise from his worry about the moral quality of that empire's headship and therefore of the Roman Empire itself, or of any empire. What would Aeneas's disobedient, furious killing have meant to the *princeps* himself? How does it complement the expected glory of Rome, present and to come?

Let me put the matter a different way while being more specific. Virgil's concern about freeing the *Aeneid* for the future might spring from the full realization of his accomplishment in unflinchingly demonstrating to us at his great poem's climax and conclusion the passion-ridden side of his hero and in suggesting what this exposition can tell us about the uses of power. At his epic's finale the poet does not put before us someone literally, or figuratively, throwing away his weapons, as Anchises asks of Pompey and, above all, of Caesar in book 6. Rather, he presents us with a vivid illustration of anger-driven vengeance at work, which is to say with a portrait of what happens when emotionality, heightened to an irrational degree, and omnipotence converge in his prime warrior's interior and exterior worlds. This account is not to the liking of those who wish to see Aeneas as a paradigm for the just and noble ruler, a model for Roman leaders to come. But it is true to Virgil's words, and it is these that have been our close companions in our own journey through one of western literature's most enduring masterpieces.

Epilogue

PROSPERO: Though with their high wrongs I am struck
    to the quick,
Yet, with my nobler reason, 'gainst my fury
Do I take part: the rarer action is
In virtue than in vengeance: they being penitent
The sole drift of my purpose doth extend
Not a frown further.

    Shakespeare, *The Tempest*, Act V, Scene 1

So what if we'd hoped to find Apollo here,
Enthroned at last, so what if a cramping cold
Chilled us to the bone. We'd come to a place
Where everything weeps for how the world goes.

    Mark Strand, "Cento Virgilianus," from *The Continuous Life*: *Poems* (1992)

I N THE FOLLOWING PAGES I speculate on the possible influence of
the *Aeneid*, and in particular its ending, on two of the masterpieces of
American literature, *Uncle Tom's Cabin*, by Harriet Beecher Stowe, and
Mark Twain's *Huckleberry Finn*.[175] I will suggest that at the moment of
the first novel's climax, when Uncle Tom is beaten by Simon Legree's
servants to the point where he can only die, Stowe's text will help us
to re-imagine how Aeneas's killing of Turnus might have appeared to
her nineteenth-century readers. I will then propose that, at the crucial
juncture in *Huckleberry Finn* when Huck tears up his letter that would
have revealed Jim's whereabouts and returned him to slavery, Twain is
deliberately answering Stowe. In the process he offers his readers an example of what they won't find at the conclusion of either *Uncle Tom's
Cabin* or the *Aeneid*, namely the restrained use of power (even, as here, in
the hands of a supposedly ne'er-do-well teenage boy) and the sparing of
someone who is already the protagonist's potential victim.

   As background, I would like to look selectively at two areas of concern.
To begin, I will examine the response to the poem's ending by two important intellectuals who lived in the centuries after the *Aeneid's* publication.
The first is Lactantius who, in the fifth book of his *Divinae Institutiones*
(*Divine Institutes*), comments at length on the question of Aeneas's piety
as he performs his final killing.[176] The second is Servius, the late antique
grammarian to whose commentary all students of Virgil are indebted.[177]
I will then leap over nearly a millennium and a half to the United States
of the early nineteenth century and to the comments of John Quincy
Adams[178] and his younger contemporary, Thomas S. Grimké.[179] With this
double set of intellectual antecedents in mind, I will return to Stowe and
Twain for a closer look at how Virgil enables us better to appreciate critical moments in their texts, and vice versa.[180]

   Let me begin with an example of Virgilian interpretation from the fifth
book of Lactantius's *Divinae Institutiones*, devoted to the idea of justice.
In it the theologian devotes several pages to an exposé of the falsity of
pagan piety. His primary target is Virgil's hero, *pius Aeneas*. I quote DI 5.
10. 1–9:

Operae pretium est cognoscere illorum pietatem, ut ex
iis quae clementer ac pie faciunt possit intellegi, qualia sint
quae ab iis contra iura pietatis geruntur. ac ne quem videar in-
clementer incessere, aliquam mihi personam poeticam sumam,
quae sit vel maximum pietatis exemplum. apud Maronem rex
ille,

> 'quo iustior alter
> nec pietate fuit nec bello maior et armis,'

quae nobis documenta iustitiae protulit?

> 'vinxerat et post terga manus, quos mitteret umbris
> inferias, caeso sparsurus sanguine flammas.'

quid potest hac pietate clementius quam mortuis humanas
victimas immolare et ignem cruore hominum tamquam oleo
pascere? sed fortasse hoc non ipsius vitium fuerit, sed poetae;
qui illum 'insignem pietate virum' insigni scelere foedaverit.
ubi est igitur, o poeta, pietas illa quam saepissime laudas? ecce
'pius Aeneas'

> 'Sulmone creatos
> quattuor hic iuvenes, totidem quos educat Ufens,
> viventis rapit, inferias quos immolet umbris
> captivoque rogi perfundat sanguine flammas.'

cur ergo dicebat eodem ipso tempore quo vinctos homines ad
immolationem mittebat:

> 'equidem et vivis concedere vellem,'

cum vivos quos habebat in potestate vice pecudum iuberet
occidi? sed haec, ut dixi, culpa non illius fuit, qui litteras
fortasse non didicerat, sed tua; qui cum esses eruditus, ignorasti
tamen quid esset pietas, et illud ipsum quod nefarie, quod
detestabiliter fecit, pietatis esse officium credidisti; videlicet ob
hoc unum pius vocatur, quod patrem dilexit. quid quod 'bonus
Aeneas haud aspernanda precantis' trucidavit? adiuratus enim
per eundem patrem et 'spes surgentis Iuli,' nequaquam pepercit
'furiis accensus et ira.' quisquamne igitur hunc putet aliquid in
se virtutis habuisse, qui et furore tamquam stipula exarserit et
manium patris per quem rogabatur oblitus iram frenare non
quiverit? nullo igitur modo pius, qui non tantum non
repugnantes, sed etiam precantes interemit.

(It is worthwhile getting to know their sort of piety [i.e., that prac-
ticed by pagans], so that from what they do in kindness and piety
we can understand the nature of what they do against the rules of

piety. To avoid the impression that I'm assailing anyone in unkindly fashion, let me adopt such a figure from poetry as seems the perfect example of piety. What lessons in justice provided that king in Vergil than whom "Never was a man more just, more pious, or more adept in warlike arts" [*Aen.* 1. 544–45]? "He had also bound behind their backs the hands of those whom he would consign to be gifts to the dead, victims whose blood would be sprinkled on the altar flames" [11. 81–82]. What can be kinder than that pious deed, sacrificing human victims to the dead and feeding the fire with human blood as if it were oil? But perhaps that was not the hero's fault but that of the poet, defaming a hero "of spectacular piety" [1. 10] with that spectacular crime. Therefore where, O poet, is that piety which you praise so very often? Behold "pious Aeneas": "Now he takes alive four warrior sons of Sulmo and four whom Ufens rears, whom he might sacrifice as offering to the shades and sprinkle [Pallas's] funeral pyre with the blood of captives" [10. 517–20]. So why did he say, at the very same moment in which he was dispatching them in chains to be sacrificed, "Believe me, I'd like to make [peace] also with the living"[181] [11. 111], when he was ordering living people, whom he had in his power, to be killed in the place of cattle? But, as I said, it wasn't the fault of him [Aeneas] who perhaps hadn't pursued his education, but of you. Though you were well-instructed, yet you didn't know what piety was. You believed that the very thing that he did so wickedly, so abominably, was the duty of piety. Plainly he is called pious for this one thing: that he loved his father. What about "the good Aeneas" who "murdered people who were offering prayers that didn't deserve to be scorned" [11. 106]? When he was entreated in his very same father's name and in his "hope in growing Iulus" [10. 524; cf. 6. 364], he spared not at all, "set aflame by the furies and [terrible in his] wrath" [12. 946]. Could anyone think that this man had any virtue in him who blazed in fury like stubble and, forgetful of the ghost of his father through whom he was implored, was unable to rein in his wrath? In no way therefore [was he] pious who killed those not only not fighting back but also in the act of prayer.)[182]

Near the end of the same century, Servius, without mention of the aspects of his hero's behavior that horrified Lactantius, would formulate what has ever since remained the standard defense of Aeneas's conduct as well as one of the principal reasons to condemn Turnus, which is to say, to put him forward as a suitable target for fully defensible emotions on the Trojan's part. Let me quote two of the commentator's final lemmas. The first is his note on line 940 (*cunctantem flectere sermo coeperat* [the speech (of Turnus) began to bend him as he hesitates]). Here are Servius's observations:

> omnis intentio ad Aeneae pertinet gloriam: nam et ex quod hosti cogitat parcere, pius ostenditur, et ex eo quod eum interemit, pietatis gestat insigne: nam Evandri intuitu Pallantis ulciscitur mortem.

[Virgil's] every purpose concerns the glory of Aeneas: for inasmuch as he considers sparing his enemy, he is shown to be pious, and inasmuch as he kills him, he wears the badge of piety, for out of consideration for Evander he avenges the death of Pallas.

What Servius does not say is that Aeneas's immediately subsequent decision not to have pity on his fallen foe transgresses the *pietas* owed Anchises and his command to spare suppliants whereas his decision to kill, though a bow to the demands of Evander, places him directly in the tradition of Achillean vengeance killings.

Let us look also at Servius's comment on line 949 and the words *Pallas inmolat* (Pallas sacrifices):

> et ad suae mortis et ad rupti foederis ultionem, te tamquam hostiam inmolat.

He [Aeneas as surrogate for Pallas] sacrifices you as a victim, both as an act of revenge for his own death and for the breaking of the treaty.

Again, when he ponders the hero's motivation, it is a double notion of revenge that Servius perceives to be paramount. And, as if he found it essential to legitimate Aeneas's action, he adds what has become the justification for it that has been often repeated in criticism ever since, namely that Turnus broke the treaty that was bartered between Aeneas and Latinus. Yet, though the Rutulian leader took advantage of Aeneas's wounding after war broke out again, it was in fact Juturna, not Turnus, first in the guise of Camers and then as originator of the omen of the eagle and the swan, who caused the renewal of hostilities.[183] If Aeneas's vengeance was directed toward Turnus as breaker of covenants, it was misplaced.[184]

But what is perhaps most striking about Servius's annotation of the epic's final lines is what the commentator omits to notice. He makes no mention of the phrase *furiis accensus et ira / terribilis*, enjambed between lines 946 and 947, and therefore of the irrationality behind Aeneas's final outburst. He likewise pays no heed to lines 947–48. There, as we have seen, Aeneas in his own words reveals the possessiveness that lies behind his emotional response to the death of Pallas. He thereby also displays how important it is to him that the living person of Turnus not be snatched from him, which is to say that he, Aeneas, not be deprived of the body upon which he could seize the opportunity to wreak his retaliation.

Let me put the point in another way. The snatching away of Turnus is not to be taken as primarily literal, even though an actual person is in question. It should not be considered parallel, for example, to Aphrodite's whisking Paris off the battlefield in *Iliad* 3 before he could be killed by Menelaus. Virgil's brilliance at this extraordinary juncture is to make the possible seizure of Turnus's body from Aeneas a psychological, not a physical, matter. It is as if some inner, spiritual virtue, such as *clementia*, were to take command of Aeneas and to allow Turnus to be sheltered from the palpability of his victor's wrath. This example of a "snatching" that is purely mental would also cause Aeneas's rage to cease and therefore allow Turnus to live, freed from his opponent's *odia*.

With these two authorities in mind I would now like to jump to the early nineteenth century and to an excerpt from one of a series of lectures that John Quincy Adams delivered at Harvard in 1806–8.[185] Adams faces squarely the same moral problematics in Aeneas's behavior, especially at his epic's conclusion, that Lactantius confronts and that Servius carefully skirts.

I quote:

> But virtue is a term so general and so comprehensive, that the idea annexed to it is seldom very precise. Aristotle therefore, after marking its universal characteristic, beneficence, the property of doing good, enters into a minute enumeration of all its parts; such as justice, fortitude, temperance, magnificence, magnanimity, liberality, meekness, prudence, and wisdom. He gives ingenious and accurate definitions of all these moral and intellectual qualities; but it deserves peculiarly to be remarked, that among the virtues he formally includes revenge. For, says he, retaliation is part of justice; and inflexibility part of fortitude. How striking an illustration is this at once of the superior excellence and of the truth of divine revelation. To mere naked, human nature, this reasoning of Aristotle is irresistible. It is not his wonderful sagacity, that deserts him; it is merely the infirmity of the natural man, in which he participates. On principles of mere natural morality revenge is a virtue, retaliation is justice, and

inflexibility is fortitude. But look for the practical comment upon this principle into the fictions of the poets; see the hero of Homer, the goddess-born Achilles, wreaking his fury upon the lifeless corpse of his valiant and unfortunate foe. See the hero of Virgil, the pious Aeneas, steeling his bosom against mercy, and plunging his pitiless sword into the bosom of a fallen and imploring enemy, to avenge the slaughter of his friend. Look for it in real history; consult Thucydides; consult the annals of the French revolution, from the instant, when that peculiar doctrine of christianity [sic], the forgiveness of injuries, was cast off, as a relic of monkish superstition; and you will trace this virtue of revenge through rivers and oceans of blood, shed in cold and deliberate butchery.

First, a word on John Quincy Adams's reading of Aristotle, which would seem parallel to the arguments used by those who draw on the Greek sage to support their defense of Aeneas's vengeful actions. I will quote only one passage (*Nicomachean Ethics* 4. 5 [1125b31–1126a2):

Now we praise a man who feels anger on the right grounds and against the right persons, and also in the right manner and at the right moment and for the right length of time. He may then be called gentle-tempered, if we take gentleness to be a praiseworthy quality. For 'gentle' really denotes a calm temper, not led by emotion, but only becoming angry in such a manner, for such causes and for such a length of time as principle [logos] may ordain; although the quality is thought rather to err on the side of deficiency, since the gentle-tempered man is not prompt to seek redress for injuries [ou timoretikos, i.e. is not vengeful] but rather inclined to forgive them.

In spite of Adams's claim, Aristotle does not praise revenge but rather the opposite. He states that the good-tempered man gets angry at the right people, for the right reasons, at the right times, and so on, but is forgiving rather than vengeful.[186] And no critic, except perhaps those like Servius who avoid the issue, would claim that Aeneas, readying himself for his final deed, was "not led by emotion," even though the cause, quality, and justifiability of that emotion may offer reasons for debate.

It is also important to remember that a major ethical touchstone for a reader of the *Aeneid* in 19 BCE to use in evaluating the morality of its hero's final actions would be not some "relic of monkish superstition" but the very Roman practice of *clementia*, which the *Oxford Latin Dictionary* defines as "a disposition to spare or pardon, leniency." There is thus no need for Adams's dubious appeal to Christianity as setting a pattern for adjudicating the behavior of Virgil's hero. It is not the "forgiveness of injuries" that is paramount here but the sparing, through the hero's restrained use of power, of an enemy brought low. This practice, or its deliberate lack, is a primary moral focus of the pages of Harriet Beecher Stowe and Mark Twain to which we will shortly turn.

With these provisos, however, we must accept the evidence of one of the most well-read of America's early presidents on how an intelligent, influential lawyer and educator understood and interpreted the conclusion of the *Aeneid* in the early decades of the nineteenth century. Adams's view would have established a powerful benchmark to guide the interpretation of readers and writers in the next decades as the United States entered a golden age of literary accomplishment.

Before turning to two masterpieces of that literature itself, let me offer one further example of how the *Aeneid* was interpreted in the period under discussion, in this case by a younger contemporary of Adams, Thomas S. Grimké, not as well-known a public figure but equally concerned with education and with the writing that was put before the impressionable young. He had a wide reputation as a speaker of consequence, and I quote from three of the orations on which his standing is based. The first is from an *Oration on American Education*:[187]

> As to their morals [i.e., of the heroes of ancient epic], who would be willing to hav [sic] a son, or brother, like the insolent and brutal Achilles, the hero of the Iliad; or like the mean and treacherous Aeneas, the hero of the Aeneid, if, indeed it has any hero.... And where is the moral of the Aeneid to be found, but in the meanness, ingratitude and perfidy of Aeneas to Dido: and in his dishonorably and forcibly depriving Turnus of his betrothed bride, against her will, and then killing him?

Or this more general statement drawn from a speech delivered in 1830:[188]

> The Bible has hitherto influenced but little the literature of modern Europe; nor do we need a stronger illustration of the fact, in regard to English Literature, than that Paradise Lost, the poem of poems, the great Scripture epic, is untaught in schools and colleges. And yet the Iliad [sic] and Aeneid [sic], far inferior as poetry, pernicious in principles and sentiments, in morals and manners, are the companions of the boy and the youth.

Or, finally, this apothegmatic utterance from an *Oration on the Comparative Elements and Dutys of Grecian and American Eloquence* where Grimké speaks of "...the coarse and insolent, the self-sufficient and half barbarian heroism of the Iliad and the Aeneid."[189]

Keeping in mind these two negative appraisals, different but complementary, dating from the preceding decades, of the *Aeneid* and especially of its conclusion, let us turn to one of the several masterpieces of American literature published in the 1850s and a major catalyst for the subsequent Civil War, Harriet Beecher Stowe's *Uncle Tom's Cabin.*[190]

I am particularly interested in chapter XL ("The Martyr").[191] Uncle Tom has aroused the special ire of his owner, Simon Legree, because he will not reveal the whereabouts of two other slaves who are runaways.

> "I *hate* him!" said Legree, that night, as he sat up in his bed; "I *hate* him! And isn't he MINE? Can't I do what I like with him? Who's to hinder, I wonder?" And Legree clenched his fist, and shook it, as if he had something in his hands that he could rend in pieces.
>
> But, then, Tom was a faithful, valuable servant; and, although Legree hated him the more for that, yet the consideration was still somewhat of a restraint to him.[192]

Already here, and elsewhere in the scene as it plays out before the climax, we have the mingling of fury, of hatred, and of the importance of possession as major themes, as they are at the end of Virgil's epic. In both contexts they are in counterpoint with the possibility that something might "hinder" the violent behavior of the person in power and urge "restraint."

The next day, however, all notions of leniency have left Legree:

> "Well, Tom!" said Legree, walking up and seizing him grimly by the collar of his coat and speaking through his teeth, in a paroxysm of determined rage, "do you know I've made up my mind to KILL you."[193]

There follows a conversation between master and slave in which Legree's rage only increases. (His roar is "like that of an incensed lion." He strikes Tom "furiously." We watch him "suppressing his rage" and speaking "in a terrible voice.")

At the culmination of the scene:

> Tom looked up to his master, and answered, "Mas'r, if you was sick, or in trouble, or dying, and I could save ye, I'd *give* ye my heart's blood;

and, if taking every drop of blood in this poor old body would save your precious soul, I'd give 'em freely, as the Lord gave his for me. O, Mas'r! don't bring this great sin on your soul! It will hurt you more than 't will me! Do the worst you can, my troubles'll be over soon; but, if ye don't repent, yours will *never* end!"

Like a strange snatch of heavenly music, heard in the lull of a tempest, this burst of feeling made a moment's blank pause. Legree stood aghast, and looked at Tom; and there was such a silence, that the tick of the old clock could be heard measuring, with silent touch, the last moments of mercy and probation to that hardened heart. It was but a moment. There was one hesitating pause, — one irresolute, relenting thrill, — and the spirit of evil came back, with seven-fold vehemence; and Legree, foaming with rage, smote his victim to the ground.[194]

Though Tom's actual death does not occur until during the subsequent chapter, the parallels with the end of the *Aeneid* are striking. In each case we are presented with two characters, one in power, the other helpless.[195] The first is in a furious rage, the second abjectly begging for forbearance. But what is focal to both episodes is a crucial pause in the action as the dominant figure, whether it be victorious hero or slave-master, delays at least for a moment before making any response, physical or otherwise, to a petition for mercy on the part of the abased.

Although *Uncle Tom's Cabin*, not unlike the *Iliad* after Achilles's slaying of Hector, continues on for five more chapters, Legree's confrontation with Tom is the climax of Stowe's novel just as the death of Turnus at the hands of a furious Aeneas is the culmination as well as the conclusion of Virgil's epic.[196] But there is one difference between the two episodes that in my view helps confirm their complementarity. It concerns the sense of sight.

To extend this extraordinary scene Stowe uses the words "moment" three times and "pause" twice, while also reflecting "silence" in the ensuing "silent," as if by repetition to stretch out for her readers what was only a flash of time. But at the core of the episode, at the center of Legree's hesitation, we watch the villain watching his victim: "...and he looked at Tom." The effect of this gaze is further to help expand the instant for the amount of time it takes the reader to survey the language that tells of it. But the sight fails to impede Legree's subsequent brutality.

However different their authors' treatment of Aeneas and Legree, it is worth pondering the parallel between the situations in which they are placed at the points of climax. The corresponding moment for Aeneas, equally impressive but anticipating an opposite result, comes at the end of his poem. We are told at lines 941–42 that the "ill-starred baldric" (*infelix...balteus*) "appeared" (*apparuit*) high on the shoulder of Turnus. The sword belt is "unfortunate" because it has already caused the death of one wearer and will soon bring about that of another. It's "appearance" is one of the links between the two killings, earlier of Pallas, now of Turnus in an act of vengeance for the first.

The baldric, of course, had been there all along, but, as Aeneas delays, it suddenly becomes powerfully personified, as if it now had a decisive life of its own when its meaning takes hold of the hesitating hero. Legree's gaze at Tom causes him to delay. Aeneas's abrupt look at the baldric, on the other hand, reminds him of Pallas and of his savage grief at his death. And after memory come only fury and a passionate stroke of the sword. By contrast, maybe even by deliberate contrast, Legree needs no memory to jog him into action, merely an innate "spirit of evil" which comes again to the fore as he smites his victim to the ground.

Let us turn, in conclusion, to another masterpiece of American literature, *Huckleberry Finn*, written and published some three decades after Stowe's novel. It, too, deals with enslavement and the master-slave dichotomy, though the relationship between Huck and the runaway Jim is quite different from that between Legree and Uncle Tom. More specifically, here, too, we have an extraordinary moment of pause during which the protagonist must make a difficult decision. Here again those seconds of hesitation are accompanied by an epiphany, with a parallel emphasis on the vision, both literal and figurative, exterior and interior, that accompanies what the sight means to its viewer. Whether or not Mark Twain understood his crucial chapter as a response, direct or indirect, to the murder of Uncle Tom one can only guess, but I will treat it as such. In it Huck becomes a hero by making a decision opposite to that of Simon Legree and of Aeneas. He chooses not to act or, rather, he opts for a symbolic deed that can only benefit the person whose life he holds in the balance.

I quote core pages from chapter 31 of *Huckleberry Finn*, entitled "You Can't Pray a Lie." Huck has already been helping the slave Jim to escape his lot. But should he continue to do so? Should he trust his own good judgment and behave in a manner that countered the hypocritical piety toward slavery that he sensed around him? He retreated to the raft "and set down in the wigwam to think."[197]

> But I couldn't come to nothing. I thought till I wore my head sore, but I couldn't see no way out of the trouble....

It made me shiver. And I about made up my mind to pray, and see if I couldn't try to quit being the kind of a boy I was and be better. So I kneeled down. But the words wouldn't come. Why wouldn't they? It warn't no use to try and hide it from Him. Nor from *me*, neither. I knowed very well why they wouldn't come. It was because my heart warn't right; it was because I warn't square; it was because I was play-ing double. I was letting *on* to give up sin, but away inside of me I was holding on to the biggest one of all. I was trying to make my mouth *say* I would do the right thing and the clean thing, and go and write to that nigger's owner and tell where he was; but deep down in me I knowed it was a lie, and He knowed it. You can't pray a lie — I found that out.

So I was full of trouble, full as I could be; and didn't know what to do. At last I had an idea; and I says, I'll go and write the letter — and *then* see if I can pray. Why, it was astonishing, the way I felt as light as a feather right straight off, and my troubles all gone. So I got a piece of paper and a pencil, all glad and excited, and set down and wrote:

Miss Watson, your runaway nigger Jim is down here two mile below Pikesville, and Mr. Phelps has got him and he will give him up for the re-ward if you send.

Huck Finn.

I felt good and all washed clean of sin for the first time I had ever felt so in my life, and I knowed I could pray now. But I didn't do it straight off, but laid the paper down and set there thinking — thinking how good it was all this happened so, and how near I come to being lost and going to hell. And went on thinking. And got to thinking over our trip down the river; and I see Jim before me all the time: in the day and in the night-time, sometimes moon-light, sometimes storms, and we a-floating along, talking and singing and laughing. But some-how I couldn't seem to strike no places to harden me against him, but only the other kind. I'd see him standing my watch on top of his'n, 'stead of calling me, so I could go on sleeping; and see him how glad he was when I come back out of the fog...and then I happened to look around and see that paper.

It was a close place. I took it up, and held it in my hand. I was a-trembling, because I'd got to decide, forever, betwixt two things, and I knowed it. I studied a minute, sort of holding my breath, and then says to myself:

"All right, then I'll *go* to hell" — and tore it up.

It was awful thoughts and awful words, but they was said. And

I let them stay said; and never thought no more about reforming. I shoved the whole thing out of my head, and said I would take up wickedness again, which was in my line, being brung up to it, and the other warn't. And for a starter I would go to work and steal Jim out of slavery again; and if I could think up anything worse, I would do that, too; because as long as I was in, and in for good, I might as well go the whole hog.

The crucial turning point, in Twain's novel as in Huck's behavior, begins when Huck says "I studied a minute, sort of holding my breath." But Twain has carefully built up to his character's words, and brilliantly stretched out the intellectual time-frame of the episode, by repeating the participle "thinking" four times followed by three instances of the word "see."

During his moment of pause Legree watches Tom at his mercy, and then pursues his violent course. Aeneas hesitates but then kills his suppliant when the belt of Pallas makes its fateful appearance for him to contemplate and then arouse him to act. Each follows a pattern from a pronouncement of hatred, to a pause, to an act of seeing, to a final brutal deed. Huck's progress has a different ending, the more powerful for the very contrast with the similar events in the works of Virgil and Stowe. Huck "sees," but what he sees is a triple vision of Jim and that vision is what causes him to shield Jim, which is to say, in his own way, to grant him his freedom. Yet Huck in fact does act, and his action proceeds from a fourth use of the verb "see": "And then I happened to look around and see that paper." From Jim he turns to the letter that, if he sends it to the slave's owner, will spell his friend's doom. "I took it up and held it in my hand." Then, after a final pause, he tears it up.[198]

Whether or not Twain meant the parallel, a reader comparing the two moments might well think of Stowe's description of Simon Legree as his violent hatred of Tom manifests itself: "And Legree clenched his fist, and shook it, as if he had something in his hands that he could rend to pieces." We turn from a metaphysical act of rending, which anticipates an actual instance of extreme brutality, to another, literal act of tearing up an object that in fact stands for something internal, the manifestation of deep spiritual quality to, and in, its performer. For in the doing is a rich act of non-doing as Huck, true hero now, permits the well-being of someone whose individuality he could just as easily take from him.

Legree, as we have seen, is ruled by possessiveness that he has in common with the emphasis Virgil gives Aeneas as he kills. Huck behaves in an opposite fashion. One of the most moving aspects of the moral victory that Huck achieves when he tears up the letter to Miss Watson is implicitly to rid himself of the notion that Jim belongs to anyone, that a human body can be someone else's property. By ripping up the letter he psychologically frees himself just as he literally frees Jim. He sees the truth of Jim's humanity, and allows him truly to live at liberty,[199] at the same time as he unchains himself from the shackles of prejudice and hypocrisy.

The classic study of interiority, in this case taking the form of an autobiographical probing into the writer's inner world, is St. Augustine's analysis of his conversion in book 9 of the *Confessions*. Twain may have had in mind this extraordinary document as he created his powerful moment of Huck's self-realization. Even if he did not it is well for readers of the *Aeneid* to keep both works, as well as *Uncle Tom's Cabin*, in mind as they ponder the conclusion of Virgil's epic. In the case of St. Augustine and of Twain's Huck the moral struggle is treated at length. The interior dialogue of Legree is adumbrated to a lesser degree, and the inner workings of Aeneas's mind that precede his final deed are only superbly suggested by his hesitation and by the moral setting in which Virgil places him where power and powerlessness play against each other. But Virgil helps us read St. Augustine, Stowe and Twain just as they in turn shed light on Aeneas's instant of innerness before he acts.

A few further comparisons are in order. Uncle Tom is viciously destroyed, and Jim is saved. But in *The Adventures of Huckleberry Finn* it is not a question of the goodness or evil of slavery that is paramount, as it is in *Uncle Tom's Cabin*, though slavery itself is often a subject throughout the novel (and no author did more than Twain to condemn its harm). Nor do we attend to one man's desperate need to take the life of another. What Twain so movingly describes is the dawning of Huck's sense of what is proper moral behavior for any individual even if that behavior seems to fly in the face of what God is said to preach. Huck's heroic courage is to act as his inner conscience dictates, and his humanity tells him that he ought to respond to his dilemma in the manner that he knows is correct, not as the supposedly pious tenets of organized religion might seem to dictate.

Let me put Huck's heroism in more universal terms. As the person in power he has the potential to use force of whatever type or dimension against that which lies within his control. To have the capability to perform a negative, even violent, action against the subservient yet dispassionately to refrain from seizing such an opportunity is, however, a mark of the true statesman. In such a situation the dominant individual becomes a paragon of temperance and self-control, of the virtue that the

Greeks as early as Homer defined as *sophrosyne*. He stands as paradigm for what is often the hardest form of valor, that of inaction.

Aeneas, too, has a choice. He can either in obedience to his father walk the impersonal path of leniency and allow his opponent to survive, or follow his inner feelings, which complement the path set out for him by Evander, and vengefully kill in a fury of wrath. Like Aeneas, Huck also follows the path of personal response. But this response, as we have said, is based on non-doing. Huck's tearing up of his letter to Miss Watson announces that he will give Jim a life, which is to say that his innate sense of right prevails even if that right seems to run against religion's accepted code as he knew it. For Aeneas not to resort to violence would be for him to accept the moral correctness of Anchises's novel pronouncement, addressed to an epic hero who happens also to be in a position to set a pattern for future behavior for a great political power, that humbled victims should not be killed, even when human nature cries out for retaliation. This is a dictum that goes as much against received heroic behavior, as canonically catalogued in the texts of Homer, as it does against man's innate propensity for anger and vengeance for hurt.

For Huck the spirit of gentleness wells up from inside as he pictures Jim and realizes the slave's dependence upon him. For Aeneas, by contrast, his father's directive would suggest an impersonal ethical pattern imposed from outside. Should he follow it, he would set a model scheme for Romans to follow. His instinctive feelings for revenge founded on furious, personal anger win out over Turnus's plea and over whatever tendency toward a moderate response his conqueror's hesitancy might have harbored.

However different they are from each other, Stowe, Twain, and Virgil are all themselves heroes for writing their respective masterpieces. Virgil's courage works in several directions. Let me conclude by suggesting two. First, it took courage to put forward as a finale the humanness of his hero, which is to say the depth of his emotionality as it works against the abstract prescriptions for heroic behavior posed earlier by father to son. At the conclusion of his epic Virgil presents to us a protagonist who exemplifies life as it is habitually lived, as we ordinarily respond to its challenges, not as it might be survived on some loftily-principled plane.

Second, and more specific, Virgil tells a hard truth to his Roman readers and specifically to Augustus, a truth that might well have deliberately reminded the emperor of ethically questionable moments in his own past, primarily when acting in the context of civil strife parallel to that of the last half of the *Aeneid*.[200] The way to power is not always morally reputable. The maintenance of power can be equally treacherous. It can even lead to the prohibited slaying of suppliants. The *Aeneid* abounds with the praise of Rome, its present and its future, and especially of the glory that will come its way under its first emperor. But at its climax and finale it also reads to Augustus, to Rome, and to us a deep lesson about our behavior which is at the same time an appeal for self-understanding. We do not conclude in a burst of praise, with peace achieved and creative life renewed. We end watching an all too available scenario: the performance of a deed of violence sparked by anger and an emotional need for retribution followed, in the poem's last line, by the resentment of him who has suffered its indignity. The narrative offers no cathartic relief, as it does in Homer's epics, whether such purgation be based on reconciliation, on lamentation for the dead, or merely on the knowledge that past ferocity may now cease. In this immediacy lies the warning that Virgil leaves to Augustus and to his legion of future students.

Afterword

DAVID RIJSER

Michael Putnam and I first met on a conference at Crete in 2008 through the courtesy of Irene de Jong and Michael Paschalis, where he delivered a splendid talk on ekphrasis in the work of one of his more recent objects of scholarly affection, Jacopo Sannazaro. Putnam's preoccupation with Sannazaro naturally flowed from his lifelong study of Virgil, and his talk on the Neapolitan poet showed with uncanny precision to what remarkable extent the latter's relation to Virgil in its turn was one of poetic affection and intimacy. Our mutual admiration for both poets soon led to further contacts, culminating in my invitation to him to come and deliver a series of lectures at the University of Amsterdam on the ending of the *Aeneid*, a subject that, apart from its intrinsic fascination, could well do with further elaboration since it had received little attention in the curriculum of our university. To my utter delight, Putnam accepted. Students and scholars were thrilled, halls were filled to the brim, and the air was resonating with Virgil. The lectures themselves were eloquent, provocative, closely argued, and inspiring. Indeed, they could only have been delivered by someone who has devoted a life of scholarship to the question at hand as Putnam has. The result of these two memorable weeks he spent talking, teaching, and discussing in Amsterdam, is in this book.

I intended the phrase "scholarly affection" above to be understood here as a *hendiadys*: for Putnam's impressive scholarship is closely intertwined with personal commitment. That scholarship itself is impeccable and of uncontested quality. Educated at Harvard in a long and distinguished tradition of classical scholarship, long time professor of classics and comparative literature at Brown University, his brilliant career has brought him many honors and awards to attest to this. His impressive production of books and articles, many about subjects related to Latin literature both antique and early modern, and many more about Virgil himself, has found a wide readership. His Virgilian bibliography is being presented in this volume as a tribute, and may speak for itself. Yet with all that, we came to know him as an extremely unassuming, accessible, easy going, cultured and polite, erudite, and inspiring friend. That extraordinary honor on our part implied, by extension, an immersion in what the poet Virgil has to say to us at the level of shared human understanding and feelings — in short, as a human being. In Putnam's reading, this is what the poet, modestly but insistently, invites us to do. And this is what his lectures convinced us of.

Putnam's work is eloquent, sensitive, and extremely intelligent. Yet for all his wide range, Putnam always returns to Virgil. His name was made with his first book, *The Poetry of the Aeneid*; in it, he began with the development of two methods: on the one hand, the search for meaning by following the track of phrases, words, and metaphorical fields to reveal "the extraordinary interconnectedness among a relatively large number of different items of experience,"[201] and on the other, the search for significance by using symbolical interpretation as a major hermeneutical tool, enlarging on the work of Pöschl. Both methods allowed him to expand a view of the epic at that time in the making. This view posits a basic bipolarity in the *Aeneid* that is formed by the constant intermingling of a panegyrical, triumphant tone, with a sorrowful, elegiac one. Putnam was one of the first to recognize the importance of the fact that the role of Aeneas's mortal enemy, Achilles, who destroyed all that was dearest to him, is the very role Aeneas is forced to take up himself at the end of the epic. This and other tragic paradoxes enabled him to draw more attention to the hitherto underestimated "dark" side of the epic. This line of criticism, kindred to that of Brooks, Parry, Clausen and W. R. Johnson, has successively become known as the "Harvard school" of interpretation. It is important to note that the critics who subscribed to that bipolarity never formed a school, and always insisted on the coexistence of both poles, the triumphant *and* the elegiac. Yet so deeply rooted was the then predominant view of Virgil as the prophet of empire on the one hand, and as the supremely rational, almost positivistic thinker on the other, that reactions from Virgilian superpowers like Roland Austin were less than jubilant.[202] That state of affairs, also necessitated a marked emphasis on the "pessimistic" aspects of the *Aeneid* to properly redress the balance. With hindsight, it now appears that many of Putnam's insights have entered mainstream Virgilian criticism, and both his methods and his conclusions have become a fundamental part of the Virgilian tradition itself.

Because Putnam has never put Virgil aside, indeed has always returned to him in his scholarly work, he develops and epitomizes here themes with which his readers are to a certain extent familiar, even the very themes with which he originally set out. These, it will appear, have deepened and ripened to a balanced and, in my opinion, incontestable view of the *Aeneid* as a tragic poem. But the care with which he has approached Virgil also exemplifies the equally fundamental awareness of the basic vulnerability of the text in the hands of the critic, who therefore must be absolutely honest and disinterested, working solely for the benefit of that text. To this attitude, then, we owe these lectures which pull together strands and threads from his whole career and thus exemplify his integrity as a critic.

This last term, *critic*, epitomizes in my view perhaps the most important facet of Putnam's work on Virgil. Classicists are often seen primarily as craftsmen, plying an academic trade. To be sure, the elucidation of ancient literature asks for expert knowledge, and indeed the rules of that game amount to a trade, the integrity and honor of which must be strenuously upheld — as they *are* upheld by the careful philologist Putnam is. But we must not forget that it is a means, and not an end. We read Latin literature, indeed all literature, because we attempt there to find insights into the nature of our lives. Ancient literature, perhaps, performs especially well in this respect, because of its distance from us, its otherness — which puts into relief all the more poignantly those elements we share with it. The veil of time through which we see antiquity suggests by its very perspicacity that its literature never could have survived if it did not contain relevance in a philosophical and aesthetic, indeed in a universal sense. Yet also, of course, this veil obfuscates. It is the balance between these two poles which is at issue in these lectures. In an age of relativism, it takes courage to accept the moral challenges the *Aeneid* still poses to us. Michael Putnam has always primarily approached Virgil, not as a classicist, however much he is one and however good he is at it, but as a reader, as a person, and as a critic, responding to the *Aeneid*'s challenges, reacting to its moral questions, and seeking for what it has to say about human life and art.

*

Putnam's readings, it has often been observed, are strongly influenced by and affiliated to New Criticism in its philological guise. In the best of that tradition, his emphasis is on the presentation of the material, of the words of the poet himself. It is characteristic of Putnam's modesty that he shuns grandiloquent interpretations of the themes he localizes so precisely within the texture of the epic. Yet what surfaces beyond doubt is that the *Aeneid*, in Putnam's reading, cannot be considered simply a panegyrical epic of Rome and Augustus. Nor, on the other hand, should it be seen merely as a subversive text. Rather, its emphatically open to interpretation, and thus, apparently, seeks for "objective" representation. Objectivity is the very term that has often been used to characterize the quality of Homer's *Iliad* to rise above a partial, Greek standpoint and to achieve an unbiased view of human life and emotions, which tries to understand and sympathize with both sides. Objectivity, also, lies at the heart of the Aristotelian tradition of interpretation of tragedy: tragedy would not be tragic without it. The descriptive force of *praxis* on the one hand, and the identification through *eleos* and *phobos* with flawed protagonists on the other hand, produce the cathartic effect of clarification and self-questioning on the part of the active and engaged spectator. Rather than moral choice or judgement, the engagement with social and cultural tensions and conflicts is at issue in Attic tragedy. Common sense, and two millennia of criticism to boot, have made us take the importance of both Homeric epic and tragedy for the *Aeneid* for granted. Of course, the idea of tragedy in Virgil was there from the start, with Martial's *Maro cothurnatus*,[203] Virgil in buskins, and the Pardo mosaic having the poet flanked by both Clio and Melpomene. Modern scholarly criticism, also, has not been remiss. Different aspects of the relevance of tragedy were shown by Heinze, Lyne, and Hardie, to name but a few.[204] Heinze and, implicitly, Lyne, have also pursued the Aristotelian connection, yet used it as a hermeneutical tool for the analysis of the "private" voice in the epic, and thus ultimately to corroborate an anti-Augustan reading. Hardie, on the other hand, persuasively endeavored to widen the focus of Virgil's interaction with tragic models from these narrower moral and psychological perspectives to a broader historical and political one, in the wake of the paradigm shift criticism of tragedy itself underwent in recent scholarship. The objective, tragic stance that might be supposed to be a logical consequence of both Homer's and tragedy's formative influences on Virgil has thus been allowed to come into view. Putnam's contributions to this process are an enormous service to Virgil, who is thus saved from the hands of those who would flatten him to the proportions of a partisan, and is rightly reclaimed as, most of all, the poet of human suffering and loss in all its inextricable complexity.

While showing us what Virgil's text is saying, Putnam through his method of pursuing the way it is saying this, points at a fundamental aspect of Virgil's method of presentation: its interrogative form. For in a very real sense, the evident lack of resolution of the epic's ending echoes, parallels, and complements the culmination of its proem, the question *tantaene animis caelestibus irae?* (1. 11). After closing the epic, that question appears to the reader as its major theme. Diachronical comparison in this case is instructive. Milton, in *Paradise Lost*, widely echoes Virgil's proem, yet declines the interrogative mode of Virgil's quoted climax, and replaces it by affirmation: "That ... I may assert eternal providence, and justify the ways of God to men" (*PL* 1. 24–26).[205] It is Putnam's great merit to point out to the reader how marked and how crucial the fact that Virgil chose to present an almost painful lack of resolution at the *Aeneid*'s ending actually is. The closure of Putnam's own text is thus fittingly presented in conjectural terms also: "What would Aeneas's disobedient, furious killing have meant to the *princeps* himself? How does it complement the expected glory of Rome, present and to come?" This shift of discursive mode, I think, is crucial for an understanding of the history of the *Aeneid*'s interpretation. For it anticipates the affirmative interpretations of many twentieth-century critics. By contrast, Virgil's emphatic questions point at the openness, objectivity, and tragic nature that Putnam seeks to posit as the *Aeneid*'s dominant theme. In the following, and as an afterthought to his remarkable book, I would like to do two things: in the first place briefly to point at the relation of the very observation that the *Aeneid* amounts to a question to the history of the interpretation of the *Aeneid*. And in the second, placing Virgil's questions within the context of Augustan Rome, to further clarify their relation to tragedy.

*

The history of the problem of the *Aeneid*'s ending is long and complicated. It was recently well discussed by Richard Thomas, and Putnam himself contributed to the theme, for instance in his introduction to his edition of Maffeo Vegio's supplement to the *Aeneid*.[206] Yet for all its complications, the essence is relatively easy to pin down. Three aspects present themselves. First, at the heart of the many misconceptions of the closure of the *Aeneid* such as Vegio's, lies the concept of poetic justice, in other words, precisely what Milton wanted to assert with his "to justify the ways of God to men." To Christian interpreters who could not willingly depart from the idea of a just and omnipotent God, artistic representation, as the reflection of His just creation, had the simple duty of illustrating the reward of the good and the punishment of the bad. However far from our modern conceptions of art, this idea empowered both the many artists who conformed to it from the Renaissance onwards, and even those fewer who, like Shakespeare, challenged it.[207] The relevance of this stance to the *Aeneid* is evident and need not be elaborated. Especially the enormous temporal extension of this line of interpretation, starting out in Late Antiquity and still discernable today, has made its presence seem almost natural. Ironically, the very openness and lack of resolution Putnam posits for the *Aeneid*'s ending, was by poetic justice transformed into closure: for with the justified killing of Turnus, who would after all be a criminal in such a view, there was indeed an end. The only thing lacking was formal, artistic acknowledgement of this justice in the form of a coda or epilogue, hence Vegio's effort. In that sense Milton's change from interrogation to affirmation contains the whole misunderstanding of antique tragedy that thwarted the development of the genre in the Renaissance.[208] For poetic justice is foreign to both Aristotle's interpretation of the working of tragedy and the practice of the Athenian dramatists that were so close to Virgil's heart.[209] Yet, with Christianity, it found its way into our cultural discourse and, detrimentally, to a Christianized Virgil.

There have, of course, always, even in the reign of poetic justice, been those like Shakespeare who saw tragedy for what it is: stark, dark, and unrelenting. The question, then, is why those have not been readers or, if so, appropriators of Virgil. This brings me to my second reason for the fact that the *Aeneid*'s ending has usually been judged problematical in the sense of unsatisfactory: the intuitive association of Virgil's epic with empire. The history of that association again is a long one, dating, so it seems, from its first reception in antiquity itself: the *Vita* of Donatus, which is universally considered to derive from Suetonius, who had access to original documents and highly reliable information, suggests as much with the phrase [the *Aeneid*] *in quo, quod maxime studebat, Romanae simul urbis et Augusti origo contineretur.*[210] Coupled with the equally reliable suggestion that the epic was written at the instigation or at least the approval of the *princeps*,[211] with the evident panegyrical aspects of its prophetic passages in books 1, 6, and 8, and with the evidence of wide spread and state-sponsored distribution of the work shortly after publication,[212] the conclusion that the *Aeneid* was what Augustus wanted is indeed hard to avoid. And what else could Augustus have wished for but praise? If so, the ending could only be construed in one way: as triumphant. And because, as Putnam shows, even the bluntest of readers must register some reserve when confronting that reading with what the text actually says, that ending was considered problematical, the usual solution being recourse to the attested unfinished nature of the epic. The triumphant and imperial reading both reflected and engendered political use being made of a foundational text. It explains the importance of what almost immediately was considered a national epic in the lives of the emperors as attested by the *Historia Augusta*,[213] and eventually, the appropriation by Dante of Virgil as the founding father and prophet of Christian theocratic diarchy by emperor and pope. From Dante the view can be shown to steadily extend itself, through the papal court at the beginning of the sixteenth century, to Ariosto and Tasso and to Milton, and from this more or less coherent reception through to the German Virgil of the nineteenth and twentieth centuries, the symbol of state and nationhood that has been so well analyzed by Schmidt.[214] There have been attempts to show that this imperial reading rests on a misappropriation of the Virgilian text by Augustus and his circle himself, that text having been almost immediately policed by a reading which in fact went against the grain of the epic.[215] I would rather suggest an alternative explanation: if we trust the antique *testimonia*, the *Aeneid* was indeed what the *princeps* wanted; and yet that same *Aeneid* contains the open and painful questions about Roman rule that Putnam has shown to be there without doubt. In that case, what Augustus wanted must have been exactly that: not a simple panegyrical text, but a layered, multi-vocal one that explained the tribulations he had sought to end, the blood of which was still damp on his hands. Such a work might include tragic conflict, even the suggestion of guilt. To accommodate that suggestion, we must of course discard or at least modify the idea of Augustus the tyrant, and move toward a more civilized, perhaps even sensitive and certainly very intelligent Augustus.

The last, and perhaps most important reason for the fact that so many readers have found the *Aeneid*'s ending problematic is also, perhaps, the most difficult to assess: the apparent lack of closure that is an important element in the argument of Putnam in this and previous treatments of this material. I would like to add to that argument here briefly because it partly converges with my last topic, the contextualization of Virgil's questions and their relation to tragedy.

*

Poetic closure is one of the main features of Western literary art.[216] Its presence or absence clearly is a crucial matter. Unsurprisingly, therefore, lack of closure in the *Aeneid* has not been conceded by all critics, as we saw above. Recent discussion on the ending has focused on two main areas of controversy, namely, first, whether Aeneas's killing of Turnus is justified or not, and in relation to the first item, and second, whether closure is accomplished or not. Pessimist critics answer both questions negatively, optimists positively. Thus Stahl sees at least three strands coming together in the killing of Turnus: the ultimate conclusion of the breach of treaty, atonement for the murder (*sic*) of Pallas and reader identification with Aeneas's savage pain for the loss of the latter.[217] Be that as it may, a cursory comparison with Virgil's main epic predecessors clearly shows the extraordinary nature of the *Aeneid*'s final chord.[218] The

Odyssey explicitly ends with the resolution of the vengeance so forcefully perpetrated by Odysseus (24. 541–48) through Athena bringing, with explicit approval of the hero (χαῖρε δὲ θυμῷ, 545) peace. The resulting civic concord is the final epitome of homecoming, resumption of the state prior to Odysseus's departure, and closure of the episode of his travels. The *Argonautica* has this same, natural cadence, the poem ending where the voyage ends. By contrast, both themes of voyage and vengeance are painfully left in suspense in the *Aeneid*. Of course, Aeneas, and the reader with him, has had forceful hints that Aeneas is "home": the Tiber's word has come true with the sow, the ships have turned to sea nymphs, the plates have been eaten. But by intertextually linking Aeneas's wanderings with those of Odysseus and the Argonauts, Virgil only brings home more emphatically than he would have done without them the very fact that a city, indeed a civilization yet to be founded, can never be a home; and by juxtaposing the Odyssean and Apollonian reminiscences with the emphatic Iliadic casting of Aeneas as Achilles, the notion of home is further and fatally problematized. As to closure, especially comparison with the *Iliad* is illuminating, as it should be, the *Aeneid*'s ending coinciding with the Iliadic themes of the later books. Of course, one of the *Iliad*'s most important themes is supplication, introduced in the negative, that is denial of supplication, in book 1, continued in this vein in book 9 and through books 16 and 22. This theme is finally resolved in book 24, where, for the first time, supplication is granted in Achilles's return of Hector's body to Priam. This resolution is magnificently sealed by the elegiac tones of Hector's funeral, which closes the epic. Both supplication and resolution are denied by Virgil. The score is clear: the comparative and intertextual paradigm in which Virgil evidently worked and thought shows his reluctance to accept traditional closure.

Yet it is important to realize that in all three cases of Virgil's epic predecessors, the closure achieved is relative, more of a truce than of a peace, so to say. Again, this is most evident with the *Iliad*: the reader knows that Troy is doomed, indeed that Hector *is* Troy, and that his funeral metonymically stands for that of the city. Putnam has shown above how Virgil exploits this connection, evoking verses that explicitly state it, *Iliad* 22. 410–11 in the finale of Dido's tragedy, 4. 669–71. It is, I think, the provisional element in the *Iliad*, and in particular the threatening presence of the future in the *Iliad*'s ending, its relativity of closure, which Virgil, as if taking hold of a small hole, has violently torn open, to reveal the gaping perspective of that very future — for that, I think, is the first suggestion evoked by his renunciation of formal closure, his reluctance to give his readers relief, his wish to present them with an open question.

The future has, of course, already been most emphatically present throughout the epic, from Jupiter's prophecy in book one, through Anchises's revelations in the Underworld, to the great ekphrastic overview of Aeneas's shield. It is not represented as an unproblematical march to triumph, but on the contrary, fraught with grief and strife, full of sound and fury — the very demons the Augustan programme of reform claimed to put at rest in the *pax Augusta*. In that sense the *Aeneid*, I would like to suggest, may be termed a do-it-yourself epic in the sense that Platonic dialogues are do-it-yourself philosophy, that is, to be supplemented by the reader himself: that Augustan peace, and the balance and closure that goes with it is for the Roman reader to achieve. And that can only be done by addressing the questions of justification, the balancing of deeds and ends that Virgil proposes by this ending, so as to awake his readers to moral maturity — which is quite something else than moral certainty or justification — in the present and the future. Virgil does this by transgressing in an almost shocking way the unity that would have been realized by traditional closure, to achieve mid-air suspension — a suspension that is seamlessly to cross over into the life and the world of the reader. Such crossovers from art to life have been shown to be an important element in Hellenistic poetics and visual art.[219] Literature and life are stimulated by Virgil to interact in a way very much akin to the Giants protruding from the great frieze of the Pergamon altar to block the path of those ascending the stairs.

In this strategy of opening up his epic to the future, the subtle mirroring of Turnus with Dido that Putnam analyses so brilliantly may also be relevant. Perhaps the most striking appearance of this phenomenon is the simile that opens book 12, set in the fields of the Carthaginians. This echo sets in motion the development of reversal in which Turnus becomes more and more frightened, vulnerable, and finally subject to the invitation to identification through the first person plural in the dream simile that Putnam points out to us in his chapter 5 above. The mirroring of Turnus and Dido not only invites comparison between two pitiful victims: it in fact connects the ending of the *Aeneid* with its virtual center, the middle of the sixth book.[220] For if Dido and Turnus are indeed so intimately related,[221] that passage contains the pendant of, and in a sense the sequel to, the theme of a final confrontation in the attempted last farewell to Dido. Virgil has thus shown us indirectly what formal closure in his hands would be like, for the scene *is* a last farewell. Yet at the same time, Aeneas's deep regrets and helpless grief show that no definitive conclusion is ever reached in emotional life. By implication, we may surmise, *mutatis mutandis*, a similar process in Aeneas's virtual subsequent handling of his act of vengeance on Turnus, his pondering whether the latter was a *superbus* to war down, or a *subiectus* to spare. Yet no more guidance of the author is obtained by the reader than oblique references, as closure is replaced by question. The reader has to do the work, and the future will decide.

This is not to say that the *Aeneid*'s ending, open as it is, lacks closural force. Formal motifs, among which rhyme and repetition (the end rhymes *sumit* and *condit* followed by *membra* and *umbras*),[222] ensure the finality of the last lines as a unit, and patterns of ring composition and thematic echoes connect the ending with the epic's beginning, thus rounding off the work as a whole: the final *solvuntur frigore membra* of Turnus echoes the same phrase used for Aeneas at 1. 92, Aeneas being *ira terribilis* in 12. 946–47 echoes the *ira* of Juno at 1.4, 11, and 25.[223] Moreover, the *Aeneid*'s ending represents an act of triumph, however fraught with moral scruple that triumph may be. Seen in this light, the amplification of Turnus's humanity and of the pathos of his fate and death add to the monumentality and iconicity of the last scene, which thus becomes a snapshot of heroism, and enables Virgil to counterbalance artistically the openness he demanded of his ending for different reasons, as we shall see. Such pathos and heroism of the vanquished is again comparable to the major frieze on the Pergamon-altar and other Pergamene monuments, where the godlike nature of the victor is implied by the heroism of the vanquished, exemplified by the dying Gauls.[224] As Philip Hardie has shown, such an act of triumph could even be configured as an act of foundation: the establishment of culture through victory.[225] Again the parallel of the commission of the Gigantomachy on the frieze of the Great Altar at Pergamon Hardie adduces is striking. It is, also in consonance with that precedent, which was after all an altar, very significant that this foundational act, the last of many cognate ones in the epic, is represented as a sacrifice. As has often been shown, sacrifice is an essential theme in the ending, as it has been throughout the *Aeneid*.[226] From sacrificant and arch Trojan Laocoon turned sacrificial victim in book 2, the scales are spectacularly and shockingly reversed as Aeneas uses sacrificial language in the final killing of Turnus, again questioning the sacral authority of the Trojan leader that had been so carefully built up in the earlier parts of the epic. The importance of the theme, and the threatening tone of its reverberations, are all the more evident with a view to Augustus, who founded his restoration of Rome on the state cult and claimed to cleanse religious practice from late Republican perversities and neglect, leading this operation in person as *pontifex maximus*. The shocking element here, as Putnam so eloquently shows, is that of *human* sacrifice, in apparently stark contrast to the pious slaughter of sacrificial beasts in contemporary Augustan practice.

The development of Turnus in books 10–12 from a violent enemy to a pitiful victim illustrates, as Putnam shows, apart from the tragic dimensions of the latter's human fate, also a reversal in role from aggressor-sacrificant to victim-sacrifice, and as such is similar to the much discussed reversal of roles Laocoon undergoes. Aristotle's ἡ εἰς τὸ ἐναντίον τῶν πραττομένων μεταβολή, the "change by which the action veers towards its opposite,"[227] has as a theme of reversal has been pursued with spectacular result by structuralist analysis of Attic tragedy.[228] In the *Oedipus Tyrannus* the protagonist starts out as almost θεοῖσι ἰσούμενος, "on a par with the gods" in 31, but ends up as the prime example of humanity being considered by the chorus ἴσα καὶ τὸ μηδέν, "next to nothing" (1187–88); he is, first, the clairvoyant, lucid intelligence, who sees all, but when all shadows are dispelled, he sees the light for the last time, unable to see or be seen. He starts as a hunter (111, 221, 475ff), ends up as the hunted (1260–65; 1451); most importantly, he turns from king into scapegoat, or *pharmakos*, necessary to procure the continuing health of the community. Knox and Vernant have assembled an astonishing number of other instances of this phenomenon in the play. This structural strategy is emphatically taken up by the *Aeneid*. Its most conspicuous appearances in the *Aeneid* are those of Aeneas who turns from victim into victor, which spans the whole epic, and of Turnus, who experiences the reverse in the last half. But the theme of reversal is constantly anticipated, for instance in the treatment of Laocoon at the beginning of book 2, where the sacrificant is notably transformed into victim. Inserted in this tale are Sinon's plausible lies, which also thematize human sacrifice, indeed, thrive upon the horror of this procedure, a horror which is shown by Sinon's capitalizing on the issue to be sympathetic to the listening Trojans. Bernard Andreae has persuasively argued for seeing the Laocoon episode as a prototype of a foundation sacrifice.[229] Laocoon's death is necessary for the foundation of Rome, because he would have prevented the Greeks from taking Troy if he would have remained alive. The connection with a foundation sacrifice is especially plausible through the emphatic religious context of Laocoon's death and his status of priest. Foundation-sacrifices, or *Bauopfer*, so it appears, are a universal phenomenon, analyzed by Sartori already in 1898, consisting of "the custom of consecrating the foundation of the city, the construction of a building ..., with the death of a human being. Usually this victim is inserted in some way in the foundation of the building."[230] The motif of foundation sacrifice in the *Aeneid* would seem to parallel that of the *pharmakos* in the *Oedipus Tyrannus*.

The motif of human sacrifice pursued by Putnam in the final books has often been subsumed under the formula *unum pro multis dabitur caput*, used to describe the impending death of Palinurus.[231] Aspects of this theme occur, apart from Palinurus, in the handling of Creusa and Misenus. Explicit association of Aeneas's rampage with human sacrifice, as the reader has seen in chapter 1 above, is abundant; it culminates in the use of *immolat* at 12. 949. In the light of this buildup of the theme throughout the epic, then, the reader is invited to see Turnus's human sacrifice as a death necessary for the foundation of Rome. Yet it is typical of Virgil's way of representing things that this necessary death is nonetheless tragic and fraught with moral scruple, with a human dimension, as Putnam argues persuasively. What is by one reckoning represented as a religious ritual by Aeneas through his use of *immolat*, is a human tragedy by another.[232] In the light of Anchises's injunctions in book 6, moreover, the legitimacy of this sacrifice is doubtful, and it has been suggested persuasively that Aeneas's sacred authority is undermined by the act.[233] Yet on the other hand it remains difficult to see if and how Aeneas could have dealt with a Turnus spared — using, in terms contemporary to Virgil, the *clementia* that eventually proved fatal to Julius Caesar.

These fundamental ambiguities are, I think, related to the function the epic was to have, and subsequently was granted, in Augustan culture: that of a unifying text, in more than one sense of the word. Much has recently been made of the consensual aspects an epic on the mythical foundation of the Roman state would inevitably have had to have.[234] Civil war had raged, victims had been made, but not all adversaries were dead, and relatives of victims survived with rancour and grief. That was no time for exultation and jubilation. To write on civil war, says Horace, is to tread on ashes under which fire still slumbers. The epic "objectivity" with which Turnus's pathos is represented could negotiate these tensions. It could provide the vanquished with honor and dignity, and moreover provide their terrible fate with significance: it was all for the good of the many, the Romans yet to come, the state as a collective. In the cosmic fusion of what appears with hindsight to be a civil war of Trojans and Latins, conflagration demands as heavy a price of life and mourning as civil war had done in the recent past of Virgil's Roman readers. Yet in both instances, from the perspective of fate, future and Jupiter, this death would, perhaps indeed should give birth to a new lease on life for Rome, to new hope: for nothing comes into existence *nisi morte aliena adiuta*, as Lucretius had it with the inimitable melancholy that so deeply seems to have influenced Virgil in his creation of Aeneas's moral dilemmata.

In this light also may be seen the *Aeneid*'s consistent theme of reversal.

As suggested, that theme was part of the literary inheritance of tragedy. But it also had arresting contingency. Aeneas fears and hates Achilles, yet has to become like his foe, and does. His first prayer is to be granted a heroic death *ante ora patrum*, yet what he does is inflict this death on Turnus, who by contrast achieves what Aeneas so ardently wished for: heroic stature. Dido, builder-queen, becomes the destroyer of her city. Turnus is first seen as an Achilles, but has to become a Hector. Hunters become hunted, sacrificants sacrificed and vice versa. The weak and destitute Trojans, losers if any there were, become the strong; and the strong, natural heroes, Turnus and Camilla, fall. All these reversals enact the paradoxes and vicissitudes of civil strife, and perhaps more importantly, enable victims to identify with and become victors. Seen from within the maze of history, we fight our sworn enemies. Seen from the Olympian perspective of Jupiter, fate and Rome, we are all part of the same great stage of human suffering, and share the world's stage, rather than being divided by it. In this sense, the *Aeneid* provides *kulturelle Gedächtnis* for a traumatized generation. It encodes lived-through horrors — though not, of course, in a direct way, but by representing the horrors of civil war as part of a mythical past, and thus part of the Roman heritage. The memorial function of the *Aeneid* is evident from its aetiological celebration of names, objects, places, and cults. But apart from that celebration, the narrative imprints another forceful "do not forget" on the reader. The oblique way in which that suggestion is administered, that is, through typological connection with the mythical past, makes what would be literally too painful and controversial, "open" to interpretation and contemplation. That very contemplation may be considered a compliment to the *Pax Augusta*.

*

Memorial and war: these are the crucial terms, implied also by the proem. But what kind of war? The *Aeneid* contains an aetiology for the Punic Wars. But in several ways Dido and Aeneas are in the first half of the epic represented as brother and sister, perhaps most conspicuously by their being compared in extended similes at structural moments to Diana and Apollo. Astonishingly, the same dynamics operate also between Aeneas and Turnus himself: these are especially triggered by the identifications with both Achilles and Hector that Virgil grants both. They share, albeit never at the same time, fields of reference as aggressors and defenders. They share, of course, courtship of the same girl. In sum, as has been observed, the more closely they are exposed to each other in the run-up to the duel, the more they seem almost to merge into one figure:[235] in that sequence, from 12. 672 onward, they are compared to boulder (Turnus) and mountain (Aeneas), and several phrases suggest their intermingling almost to indiscrimination (*coisse*, 709; *miscetur in unum*, 714).

Through the epic objectivity of the *Aeneid*, and Virgil's constant reminders of the intermingling of roles that both have to play first separately, then "rolled up into one ball" in the duel, Aeneas and Turnus thus become, again seen from above and from a distance, and not in the heat of the brawl, congenial rather than adversary — as those who fight a civil war all are in the last reckoning. This aspect is strikingly illustrated by two intertextual references in the climax of the sequence under scrutiny: the simile in 715–22 illustrating the coming together of Aeneas and Turnus. The image of the two bulls fighting for leadership and their wavering spectators to which the combatants and their public are compared not only eliminates distinction between them, but intertextually refers to Ennius's description of the fight between Romulus and Remus, *omnibus cura viris uter esset induperator*.[236] The reference, then, is to civil strife. Yet again, this is not all. For Virgil's simile also points once again to tragedy, in this case Sophocles's *Trachiniae* 508–22. If not the marked tragic content of the epic, at least its continuous allusion both to themes and concrete passages of tragedy has of course been widely acknowledged.[237] It is perhaps illuminating in this context to point to the fact that these tragedies had functioned as a civic ritual, negotiating social, personal, and political tension and creating, through the coupling of opposites and the submission of these to a larger whole, consensus: if different moral, political, and, indeed, existential attitudes were opposed to each other in these plays, as they are for instance in the *Antigone*, these were watched and scrutinized by the Athenians *together*, the performance thus uniting both poles as accommodated by the rich and varied culture of Athens. It is to this role, I think, that the *Aeneid* aspires as well. And in this functional sense the epic is the Roman complement, not only to the epics of Homer but to Attic tragedy, also. If such a work was what Augustus wanted, this surely coincided with his marked adoption of Athenian motifs of his patronage in visual art.

The Athenian connection may help to explain what induced Virgil to so completely merge the epic and tragic genres. Tragedy there was, as the examples of Pollio and Varius attest. But Virgil's epic seems to have superseded them. The simple *Kreuzung der Gattungen* is perhaps no sufficient explanation;[238] nor will the traditional Roman combination of tragedian and epicist suffice. Other factors that led Virgil to have epic perform the social and political function of tragedy may be the plebean and populist nature of theatrical performances in the late Republic, its song and dance and quite untragic character (of which Augustus, by the way, seems to have been fond as well), its all too concrete visualization of political reality by seating arrangements; all combined to cause that traditional tragedy, as it has been termed, struggled to keep attention.[239] A significant factor may also be the approximation of the two genres through the increasingly recitational practice of both. But the most important, it seems to me, is the realization that the tragic in the Aeneid is not merely, or even primarily, "generic enrichment" through the presence of echoes and handlings of tragic themes.[240] The emphatic evocation of tragic context from beginning to end — Juno's wrath, the theater in Carthage at the beginning, the theme of the Furies and Turnus's and Aeneas's tragic reversals at the ending — serves a larger purpose than literary or intertextual appropriation of the genre: it helped to suggest that Augustan Rome was the incarnation of Periclean Athens.[241]

To return to Virgil's allusion to Ennius: seen in this light, the ultimate consequence of a tragic and objective interpretation of the epic is to interpret the killing of Turnus on a symbolical level as fratricide. Fratricide, again, was an eminently tragic theme, especially in connection with the Theban cycle. Its importance in the Athenian plays may very well have been innovative and must, I think, at least partly be seen in the light of tragedy's function of stabilizing through visualization social and political pressures and conflicts in the community. Yet in a Roman context, the perspective of fratricide causes the Aeneid's ending to become a typological counterpart to the other foundational myth of Rome, the killing of Remus. T. P. Wiseman has connected the origins of the Remus myth in his wonted controversial way with human sacrifice perpetrated by the Romans to avert the crisis of the Samnite and Etruscan wars in 296 BC.[242] He has not met with much scholarly approval, and the thesis is highly speculative. But what Wiseman did show convincingly, was the connection of the traditional foundation myth of Rome, the killing of Remus, with foundation sacrifice. It is very tempting to see in the last scene of the Aeneid a reflection of that myth. The last act of the trilogy of fratricide, of course, had been acted out briefly before Virgil started writing: Augustus and Antony were brothers through marriage, and the civil war they fought had brought disaster in an unprecedented way. That disaster, Virgil suggests, was portended by the cruelty and terror of the Aeneid's ending and its re-enactment at Rome's second foundation by Romulus. Thus the final act of the Aeneid is at one and the same time in religious terms a foundational sacrifice wherewith Rome begins, but as such also, in human terms, a tragedy. With such beginnings, the painful and difficult history of Rome, culminating in devastating civil war, could be seen as atonement, and Virgil's depth of understanding of human suffering in the *Aeneid* as a magnificent and moving cry for deliverance.

Notes

1   The word *inermem* (311) is particularly telling, given the emphasis on Aeneas's arms in the epic's final lines.

2   *Aen.* 12. 311-12 (*At pius Aeneas dextram tendebat inermem / nudato capite...*).

3   The philological problems connected with *Aen.* 2. 566-88 are discussed below at ch. 3, n. 94.

4   I analyze in detail these important lines (*Aen.* 6. 851-53), and speculate on the reason for Virgil's use of hysteron-proteron in the order of the infinitives, in Putnam (2005), 453-75, especially 459-60.

5   *Aen.* 10. 514. Turnus is also called *superbus* at 12. 326 as he returns to battle after the wounding of Aeneas.

6   It is a commonplace of Virgilian criticism that the second half of the *Aeneid* retells aspects of the plot of the *Iliad*. It is also now more readily accepted than in the past that in the same narrative progress Virgil suffers his hero to become a version of Achilles *redivivus*.

7   When Achilles addresses Lycaon as φίλος (*Iliad* 21. 106) as he is about to kill him, his apostrophe is unlikely to be meant sympathetically. Since in the narrator's introduction to his speech his voice is called ἀμείλικτον (harsh, cruel), the reader presumes an ironic tone to his word. I deal with the Lycaon episode in detail in chapter 1.

8   See *Aeneid* 1. 294.

9   *Aeneid* 7. 37.

10   *Aeneid* 10. 160-61. At 5. 852 Virgil uses the cognate accusative construction with *adfixus*.

11   For an indirect parallel between Aeneas and Achilles in the first six books we might compare the simile at *Il*. 22. 410-11 with its imitation by Virgil at *Aen.* 4. 669-71. In the first, the death of Hector prefigures the ultimate burning of Troy. (The interdependence of Troy and Hector is a subject for discussion between the hero and his wife at *Il*. 6. 407-65.) By causing the death of Hector, Achilles initiates the former city's doom. In the second simile, the death of Dido, and the mourning that accompanies it, are compared to the destruction of Carthage itself. By deserting Dido and instigating her suicide, Aeneas sets in motion the ruin of Carthage as well as its queen. I will deal in chapter 4 with the notion of Aeneas as city-destroyer.

12   The reader compares this general statement with Anchises's earlier command, specifically to Caesar to "spare" (*parce*, 6. 834) and to dispense with his weapons (*proice tela*, 835).

13   We note also Turnus's *iussa superba* at 445 and Pallas's astonishment at them, and his posture *super adsistens* (490) after he has killed Pallas.

14   Compare also the several uses of *dextra* that dot the verses of *Aeneid* 8, among

them 124, 164 (where the use is double), 169, 467, and 558. The verb *debere* leaves it implicit that, at least in his eyes, the life of Turnus is due Evander in recompense for the death of Pallas.

15 Homer *Il.* 11. 67-69; cf. Apollonius *Arg.* 3. 1187. The parallels are noted by Harrison (1991) on 10. 513-14.

16 Lyne (1989), 155-56.

17 Catullus never uses the simple verb *meto*. We note also the appearance of the form *ferro* in the subsequent lines of both poems.

18 The first major connection between Aeneas and Achilles in book 10 is actually through the parallel between 10. 270-71 and *Iliad* 18. 205-6, when Achilles makes ready to reenter the fighting. There follows a simile of smoke going up from a beleaguered city. (The student of Virgil, knowing his Homer, might expect something parallel of Aeneas, soon to besiege Latinus's city.) The ancient reader would expect something equivalent to follow in the *Aeneid*. But Virgil offers a different, double simile at lines 272-75:

> non secus ac liquida si quando nocte cometae
> sanguinei lugubre rubent, aut Sirius ardor
> ille sitim morbosque ferens mortalibus aegris
> nascitur et laevo contristat lumine caelum.

> ...just as when in the clear night comets glow blood-red and baneful; or as fiery Sirius, that bearer of drought and pestilence to feeble mortals, rises and saddens the sky with baleful light. (Fairclough-Goold)

Virgil's only other mention of comets is at *Geo.* 1. 488, where their appearance prefigures the disaster of Roman civil war when Emathia twice grew rich "with our blood" (*sanguine nostro*, 491, repeated at 501).
The origin of the second part is *Iliad* 22. 26-31. Achilles, as Priam watches, is:

> ...like to the star that cometh forth at harvest-time, and brightly do his rays shine amid the host of stars in the darkness of night, the star that men call by name the Dog of Orion. Brightest of all is he, yet withal is he a sign of evil, and bringeth much fever upon wretched mortals.

With Sirius, the Dog Star, in Canis Major, cf. Mezentius as Orion, the hunter accompanied in the heavens by his dog, at 10. 763-67. Aeneas and Mezentius have their parallels. Cf. also the mention of Sirius at 3. 141-42:

> ...tum sterilis exurere Sirius agros,
> arebant herbae et victum seges aegra trahebant.

> ...then Sirius burned the fields barren, the grass dired up and sickly crop denied its yield.

The connection here is with the abortive foundation on Crete (we note *aegra... corpora* at 3. 140-41). The arrival of Aeneas in book 10 bodes ill for both people and place. Aeneas is thus at once symbol of the horrors of civil war and of Achilles about to destroy Hector and Troy.

19 It should be remarked here, and also in connection with the slaying of Turnus at the poem's end, that the vengeful violence which Aeneas now displays is, on first impression, incongruous as a reaction to the death of a single hero, one whom Aeneas has met for the first time just a few days previously, whatever the obligations that might exist between Aeneas, the slain warrior, and the latter's father. The fact that Achilles and Patroclus have known each other since boyhood (for their age differential see *Iliad* 11. 780-90) explains the depth of the former's response far more readily. The reasons for Aeneas's exaggerated reaction only become clearer at the poem's denouement (see especially chapter 6 below).

20 The language is the same as 18. 336-37, with one minor change.

21 Guilt may play some part in explaining the ferocity of Aeneas's actions, but it is the differences in Virgil's transference of Achilles to Aeneas here that catch the attention. Achilles is doubly motivated by heroic anger and by his love for Patroclus, whom he has known since boyhood. By contrast, Pallas is much younger and has been in Aeneas's life for only a brief while.

22 The ultimate result of Aeneas' "anger" is the foundation of Rome. It is the degree of his anger within the context of the poem that disturbs the reader.

23 If the human victims were burned we never hear of it. For the slitting of an animal's throat in sacrifice, see also *Aen.* 12. 214. Aeneas's killing of Mezentius by the same means brings book 10 to an effective conclusion.

24 See the valuable article by MacKay (1999, 89) for appreciation of the importance of the Lycaon episode for the career of Achilles. MacKay doesn't discuss Virgil's imitation of the episode, since that would argue against his interpretation of Aeneas as someone who has "outlived almost the sense of personality.... [He is] a man with a public, not a private mission...." Cf. Parry's remark, in an equally influential article, that "The private voice, the personal emotions of a man, is never allowed to motivate action" (1999, 63).

25 *Dextram* (3. 610). Achaemenides's posture as suppliant had been made clear at 592: *supplex...manus ad litora tendit* (as a suppliant, he stretches his hands toward the shore).

26 Virgil also puts the phrase *gnatoque patrique* into the mouth of Evander (11. 178) and thus pits the two pieties against each other.

27 The jingle *...am laeva* appears in the same metrical position in the previous line in each case (2. 552, 10. 535). We should compare also the description of Aeneas's subsequent killing of Lausus (10. 815-16):

> ...validum namque exigit ensem
> per medium Aeneas iuvenem totumque recondit;...

> ...for Aeneas drives his stout sword straight through the youth and buries it completely.

The Fairclough-Gold translation adds the phrase "to the hilt," which is not in the Latin.

28 *Ara* (513, 514); *altaria* (515, 550).

29   If the behavior of Achilles should here become a norm for the morality of Aeneas's actions, as Virgil now most intensely patterns his hero's deeds after that of the *Iliad*'s protagonist, then he fails even to meet this Homeric standard of behavior.

30   We have come a long way from the Aeneas who reacts to the scene of ransom that he sees depicted by Dido's artisans on the walls to her temple to Juno (*Aen.* 1. 483-87):

> ter circum Iliacos raptaverat Hectora muros
> exanimumque auro corpus vendebat Achilles.
> tum vero ingentem gemitum dat pectore ab imo,
> ut spolia, ut currus, utque ipsum corpus amici
> tendentemque manus Priamum conspexit inermis.

Three times Achilles had dragged Hector around the walls of Troy and was selling the lifeless body for gold. Then indeed from the depths of his heart he utters a mighty groan as he beheld the spoils, the chariot, the very corpse of his friend, and Priam stretching forth his weaponless hands.

Aeneas will take the same position at the ethical highpoint in book 12 (*At pius Aeneas dextram tendebat inermem*, 311), the last occasion in the poem that he is called *pius* as he calls for an end to the anger (*iras*, 314) of those battling. There is no sign of groaning as he prepares to kill the suppliant Magus who, like Priam, had also offered ransom.

31   We should remember, however, since Pyrrhus's behavior is focalized through the words of Aeneas, not of Virgil, that the ethical benchmark against which his actions are measured is that of the recounting hero, not of the writer. It is Aeneas who paints a darker vision of Pyrrhus than is perhaps necessary. Unlike the epic bard, he is incapable of distancing himself from events in which he had participated. Nevertheless, his words to Dido center on Pyrrhus's anticipation of Virgil's own treatment of Aeneas's behavior at the conclusion of the poem, just as they foreshadow that of Augustus during civil war.

32   Virgil connects the deaths of the eight human sacrifices and of Haemonides with that of Turnus by his only uses of the verb *immolare* (10. 519 and 541; 12. 949). As we will examine in the last chapter, the death of Turnus is one final human sacrifice.

33   On Philodemus and the anger that "inspires one to commit sacrilege, insulting the priests, and outraging suppliants…," see Fish, 122. Aeneas's conduct goes a grisly step beyond insult and outrage.

34   For the *tropaeum* in the *Aeneid*, see Nielson, and Dyson (146-47, 184-94); for more general treatments, see Hölscher and Hope.

35   For more information, see Burke.

36   In each case, the narrator apostrophizes Mars. The wording at 10. 542 is *tibi, rex Gradivus, tropaeum*, at 11. 7-8 it is *tibi magne tropaeum / bellipotens….*

37   Modern Palestrina, to the southeast of Rome.

38   The only other time that Virgil gives Aeneas the epithet is at *Aen.* 12. 775. Dardanus's origin at Corythus is mentioned at 3. 170 and 7. 209.

39 The structure of *Aen* 7. 678-81 is extraordinary in that three full hexameters pass before we learn that Caeculus is the subject of his sentence and, when his name at last appears, it comes during enjambment and both begins a new hexameter and initiates a sense pause. We are being readied for the reappearance of his name.

40 Three out of the twelve chief heroes singled out in the catalogue of book 7 are killed by Aeneas in book 10 (Caeculus, Umbro, Mezentius). The sons of another, Ufens, are taken for human sacrifice. Turnus is saved for the final death.

41 *Aen* 7. 760 offers powerful evidence in support of those who believe that Virgil purposefully left certain lines incomplete for their poetic effect.

42 *Marsis...montibus* (7. 758) is echoed by *Marsorum montibus* (10. 544).

43 The phrase *multa parantis / dicere* is a variation of *multa parantem / dicere* at *Aen.* 4. 390, where *dicere* is enjambed between lines. (These are Virgil's only uses of the phrase.) The parallel suggests an important reversal of roles. In book 4 Aeneas is attempting to cope with Dido who, a few lines before, has characterized herself as *furiis incensa* (4. 376). In book 10, it is Aeneas who rages (*furit*, 545) while Tarquitus plays Aeneas's part as pleader against the irrational.

44 The phrase *ad litora* at 10. 574 is the nearest reminder.

45 For the connection of this passage with the early career of Augustus, when he was still known as Octavian, see Putnam (2002), 118.

46 As did Servius and ServiusD when commenting on 2. 557, we think of the death of Pompey (on which, see, most recently, Berno). But the commentator also mentions a version of the story of Priam's demise used by Pacuvius, which he tells in his note on line 506. Troy's king "was captured by Pyrrhus in his own home but was dragged to Achilles's funeral mound and killed next to the promontory of Sigeum, for Achilles was buried at Rhoeteum; then Pyrrhus carried around his head impaled on a stick." Pacuvius's exactitude may in part elucidate Virgil's splendidly opaque use of *litore*. In *Aeneid* 10, Tarquitus's death on the shore of the Tiber helps explain why his corpse would be available either to birds, or fish, or both.
For further detail, see Austin (1964), introductory note to 506-58 and on 557.

47 The repetition of *caput* and of forms of *truncus* and *iaceo* further presses the parallel.

48 With *patrem qui obtruncat ad aras,* cf. 3. 332 where Aeneas describes Pyrrhus's own death at the hands of Orestes (*patrias...obtruncat ad aras*). The theme of vengeance, in particular because of love lost, is operative here. Hermione had been betrothed to Orestes, but her father, Menelaus, gave her to Pyrrhus instead. Virgil's repetition suggests that Pyrrhus's death can also be seen as an act of revenge for his ugly killing of Priam. (The phrase *ad aras* implies that Achilles's son was now himself in the position of suppliant. He is also *incautum* [3. 332].)

49 Virgil never uses the word *supplex* of Priam when confronting Pyrrhus, but his position at the altars and his chiding of Pyrrhus for not respecting the rights of a suppliant as did his father Achilles when Priam was a suppliant for Hector's body (*Aen.* 2. 541-42) make clear his suppliant posture in *Aeneid* 2.

50 The relationship between a truncated victim and the *tropaeum* needs to be further pursued, especially in relation to Aeneas's making of the *tropaeum* of

Mezentius at the beginning of book 11. His act of manufacture creates a visible, monumental, artistic accomplishment that in this case gives permanence to the brutality of vengeance. We begin with Priam as *truncus* and make our way to Mezentius as *tropaeum*. We never learn whether Aeneas decapitates Mezentius or what he does with the body. His weaponry becomes part of Aeneas's craftsmanship. (Virgil does use the vague *sinistrae* at 11. 10 to denote the left side of the trunk reflecting the former body.)

51 *Iliad* 1. 401-6.

52 *Theogony* 147-53; 713-35.

53 *Hymn to Delos* 141.

54 Cf. the *Sirius ardor* (10. 273) to which Aeneas's helmet peak is compared (*ardet*, 270) and the flame and fire that spew from its top as well as from his shield (the helmet is also shown as "spewing flames" [*flammas...vomentem*] at 8. 620). It is not coincidental that the monster Cacus in book 8 is seen "spewing black flames from his mouth" (*atros / ore vomens ignis*, 198-99) and later "spewing vain fires" (*incendia vana vomentem*, 259).

55 Horace uses the verb at *Epi* 1. 3. 14, a work being written contemporaneously with the *Aeneid*.

56 Comment on line 574.

57 Cf. *Aen.* 1. 474-78.

58 To which ServiusD adds *aut e longinquo* ("or from a distance"). This is the way the phrase is taken by some critics, e.g., Williams (1973) on line 572 ("coming from afar").

59 For this and further examples, see Maltby, s.v. Gradivus. Though ancient, the etymology of *Gradivus* (from *gradior)* is false. The "i" is long in the first, short in the second.

60 Seneca or [ps.]Seneca has the phrase *dirum fremens* twice (*Oed.* 961, *H. O.* 1679) and Silius (*Pun.* 4. 378) has *dira fremunt*. Cf. also Apuleius *Met.* 8. 11.

61 We first hear of the Dirae in the *Aeneid* at 4. 473 and 610, in both cases styled *ultrices*.

62 Harrison (1991), on lines 576-77, notes the chiastic pattern.

63 The opening out of the breast with the sword-point is another particularly gruesome detail. Pease (on *Aen.* 4. 63, *reclusis*) quotes Silius 1. 119-22, but the lines speak with equal aptness to *Aen.* 10. 601 because of the common presence of *anima*:

> ...tum nigri triformi
> hostia mactatur divae, raptimque recludit
> spirantes artus poscens responsa sacerdos
> ac fugientem animam properatis consulit extis.

> ...then a black victim was sacrificed to the goddess of triple shape; and the priestess, seeking an oracle, quickly opened the still-breathing body and questioned the spirit, as it fled from the inward parts that she had laid bare in haste.

Aen. 4. 63-64 are quoted by Macrobius (*Sat.* 3. 5. 2) as part of a discussion of the offering of the *anima* of a sacrificial victim to a god. See below for Virgil's final use of *recludo*, at *Aen.* 12. 924, as Aeneas's spear opens out Turnus's corselet.

64 Most editions print *campi*, the suggestion of Achilles Statius (Aquiles Estaço) in his edition of 1566. It is confirmed by *Ilias Latina* 384 (*sanguine Dardanii manabant undique campi*). See M. Scaffai, ed., *Baebius Italicus: Ilias Latina* (Bologna, 1997), on 384f. Cf. also the language of Statius *Ach.* 1. 84-89.

65 At *Aen.* 6. 89 the Sibyl speaks of *alius Achilles* that Aeneas will confront in the wars to come. The language clearly applies to Turnus, but by the end of the poem her words must also be taken, prophetically and proleptically, of Aeneas himself.

66 The first analogy is also appropriately drawn from *Iliad* 5. 87-8 at the start of the *aristeia* of Diomedes that soon leads to his duel with Aeneas.

67 *Recludit* (10. 601, 12. 924).

68 *Precantis* (10. 598), *dextram precantem* (12. 930).

69 *Miserere* (10. 598, 12. 934).

70 12. 311-14.

71 The phrase *iustae irae* at *Aen.* 10. 714, used as a predicative dative, also addresses the propriety of an angry response to Mezentius's villainy.

72 See also Putnam (1995), 134-51.

73 Williams (1973), e.g., *ad loc*, opts for the first sense ("and the picture of his love for his father came into his thoughts"), Harrison (1991), *ad loc.*, for the second ("Here *patrius* must be objective, 'shown towards his own father'"). Both refer to 9. 294 (*et mentem patriae strinxit pietatis imago*).

74 *Aen.* 12. 545.

75 When Aeneas leaves Buthrotum, Helenus offers him, as a host's parting gift, the "arms of Neoptolemus-Pyrrhus" (*arma Neoptolemi, Aen.* 3. 469). The irony of the gesture only becomes fully apparent as the epic progresses. We learn from Homer that a person who dons someone else's armor often becomes, to whatever degree, that other person. (For the dangers inherent in donning someone else's armor, see Hornsby [1966].) We never hear that Aeneas actually puts Pyrrhus's weaponry to use. Merely their possession by Aeneas helps propose the equation between the two that Virgil's text fosters by other means.

76 See also ch. 1, note 11.

77 A recent, searching discussion of the ekphrasis is to be found in Rijser, xviii-xxii. See also Putnam (1998), 23-54, and its bibliography.

78 I am treating the ekphrasis as both a frozen depiction of the past, to be remembered by the viewer-reader, and as active and proleptic for events in the future. The authority of art bestows immortality through the confirming power of its patterning. But, at least through the flexibility of Virgil's magic, the fixity of visual art is complemented and magnified by the creative fluidity of verbal nuances.

79 Penthesilea will reappear later in simile when she and Camilla are compared (11. 659-63). The conclusion of 1. 490 is directly echoed at 11. 663. Nearer to hand, the phrase *aurea subnectens* (1. 492) is echoed in the description of Dido preparing for the hunt (*aurea...subnectit*, 4. 139). It will also not be long before Dido also is frenzied (*furens*, 4. 69) and burns (*ardet*, 4. 101).

80   As David Rijser reminds me, the subsequent simile (498-502), comparing Dido to Diana, deliberately recalls *Odyssey* 6. 102-8, where Nausicaa, on first meeting the epic's hero, is compared to Artemis. Virgil thus introduces an elegant juxtaposition at this point in book 1 (Aeneas is for a moment both Achilles and Odysseus) and with it a tension in the narrative whose resolution the reader now awaits. Will Aeneas prove to be the first or the second?

81   *Donum* or *dona*: 1. 652, 659, 679, 695, 709, 714; 2. 31, 36, 44, 49, 189. *Doli*: 1. 673, 682, 684; 2. 34, 44, 62, 152, 196, 252, 264. With *cingere flamma* cf. 9. 160 and 10. 119 (*cingere flammis*), of the Trojan camp under siege, and 3. 52, of Troy itself (*cingi...urbem obsidione*).

82   See 1. 754 and 2. 36, 65, 310 for *insidiae* as part of Troy's ruin.

83   As 4. 77-79.

84   It is worth noting how *quantus deus* (719), which is descriptive of Cupid, is absorbed into *quantus Achilles* (752) as Aeneas begins his tale.

85   Four lines previously (326) Dido described herself as potentially *captam* in conjunction with the taking of her city.

86   Austin (1964) (on 4. 466ff.) is correct to remind us of another instance of a dream (12. 908-12), which I examine in more detail below. There Turnus is seen as helpless before the force of the *dea dira* (12. 914) sent by Jupiter but whose instrument is also Aeneas. The parallel between the two episodes is reinforced by the simile that follows in book 4 (469-73), where Dido is compared to Pentheus or Orestes pursued by Furies (the simile runs its course masterfully, framed by *Eumenidum* and *Dirae*). The subsequent line (474) adds to the horror when we learn that Dido "conceived Furies" (*concepit furias*).

87   The translation is by Austin (1964) (on 4. 71). I will deal with the simile in greater detail below.

88   *Arg.* 4. 1452-53.

89   In the lines that immediately follow, Aeneas is compared to a *nimbus* and the destruction that it brings to the farmers' ordered world.

90   Austin's note (1964) on 4. 669 is typically sensitive: "For Dido's death means the death of her own Carthage, and it foreshadows the ultimate destruction of the city; and the sack of Troy is an ever-present memory."

91   Cf. also *urbs antiqua ruit* (2. 363).

92   I will comment later on the similarities of both passages with the death of Amata at 12. 604-7.

93   *Genetrix pulcherrima* (12. 554).

94   The authenticity of the "Helen episode" has been much discussed. The lines in question (2. 567-88) are preserved in the *vita* of Servius to be found at the start of his *Comentarii*, where they are said to have been deleted by Tucca and Varius, Virgil's literary executors. The comment is reiterated by ServiusD on *Aeneid* 2. 566 and by Servius on 2. 592. In his note there which refers specifically to 2. 601 (*hinc autem versus esse sublatos, Veneris verba declarant dicentis "non tibi Tyndaridis facies invisa Lacaenae"*), Servius acknowledges that an omission has taken place between lines 566 and 589. As one connection between 567-88 and what follows, we might note that Virgil's only two uses of a form of *Tyndaris* are at 569 and 601.

I follow those, from de la Cerda in the seventeenth century to Austin (1964, on

Aen. 2. 567-88; see especially pages 217-19, with mention of Austin's own important treatment [1961]) and Williams (1972, on *Aen.* 2. 567f.), among others, in
the twentieth, who accept authenticity for the passage. There is one incontro-
vertible argument in its favor. The narrative starting at line 589 of the manuscript tradition makes no sense without it. The reader cannot jump from line
566 to line 589 and then be expected to understand why Venus has to bridle the
angry fury of Aeneas. Most recently, Horsfall (2008) offers a detailed argument
against authenticity (553-86).

For a different argument in favor of authenticity, see Fish, 111-38, especially
120-21 and 125-29, and 135, n. 59, for an up-to-date bibliography on the subject.

95 In line 587, I read *flammae* for *famam*, the reading of the manuscripts of Servius.

96 Of the many further interconnections between Venus's speech and the preceding narrative, perhaps the most vivid can be drawn from lines 601-2: "It is
not the features of Helen, hated by you, or wicked Paris..." (*non tibi Tyndaridis
facies invisa Lacaenae / culpatusve Paris,...*) who are to blame for Troy's ruin but
the unforgiving nature of the gods. As we have seen, *Tyndaridis* looks back to
Tyndarida (569). *Invisa* also recalls *invisa* (574), and *facies* is a vivid reminder
of the vision of Helen, illuminated by the fires of Troy, which Aeneas has just
experienced (*aspicio*, 569).

97 *Ira* (4, 11, 25, 130, as well as 251).

98 Cf. 592-93 (*dextra...prehensum / continuit*).

99 *Arae* (514), *altaria* (515).

100 Cf. 10. 519 and 541.

101 *Aen.* 12. 554. The change from the Venus who, in book 2, urges her son to forget
about revenge and depart piously from Troy's ruin, to the Venus who sends him
the notion of destroying Latinus's city is not without sharp irony.

102 Virgil suggests several other parallels between the arrivals in Carthage and at
the mouth of the Tiber. With 1. 376 (*per aequora vectos*) cf. 7. 65 (*trans aethera
vectae*, in the omen quoted fully below), and 228 (*per aequora vecti*). We think
also of balancing mentions of the *Belli portae* at 1. 294 and 7. 607, and of the
portraits of Aeneas given by Ilioneus at 1. 544-45 and 7. 234-35. At 1. 647-55
we saw that Aeneas offers as gifts to Dido a cloak of Helen and the scepter of
Ilione, which is to say intimations of adulterous love and suicide. At 7. 245-48 he
offers Latinus a goblet belonging to Anchises and the *gestamen* (scepter, tiara,
and robes) of Priam. This inheritance from the rulership and fate of Troy will
also fulfill its ominous overtones.

103 The negative tone Virgil gives the word *advena* begins at *Ecl.* 9. 2-3, where an
advena possessor has proscribed the shepherd's land. At 4. 591 Dido in bitterness styles Aeneas an *advena*. Finally, the augur Tolumnius, as he urges his colleagues to recommence the war, calls Aeneas an *improbus advena* (12. 261).

104 On the etymological connection between the two words, see Williams (1973) on
7. 69-70.

105 The word *casus* also plays on its direct etymology from *cadere*, to fall.

106 I have dealt elsewhere with the relationship of *fumantia culmina* with *culmina
fumant* (*Ecl.* 1. 82) as a unifying factor for Virgil's total oeuvre. See Putnam
(2010), 33-34.

107 *Aen.* 4. 669-71. See also ch. 3, p. 59.

108 Compare the positive purpose of the beekeeper's use of smoke at *Geo.* 4. 230 (*fumos...manu praetende sequacis*). At *Iliad* 18. 109-10 Achilles equates smoke with anger.

109 The closest parallels to the phrase in Virgil are *ceu fumus in auras* (*Geo.* 4. 499), of the spirit of Eurydice, and *tenuis ceu fumus in auras* (*Aen.* 5. 740), of the ghost of Anchises.

110 The whole simile is quoted above, ch. 3, p. 57.

111 *Miratur*, twiceover (1. 420-21), in anaphora.

112 See also ch. 2, p. 45.

113 See, e.g., Williams (1972) on 2. 304f.

114 We note also that Virgil adds fire as a second element of destruction to Homer's water.

115 "Hunting, whenever it is mentioned, represents either a specially motivated excursion from the pastoral proper, as in [*Ecl.*] 2. 29 and Th[eocritus] *Id.* 11. 40-1, or as here [*Ecl.* 7. 29] and in 10. 55-7 an infusion of the real countryside into the myth" (R. Coleman, ed., *Vergil: Eclogues* [Cambridge, 1977], on *Ecl.* 7. 29).

116 *Incessi muros, ignis ad tecta volare* (12. 596).

117 The parallels begin in book 7, where the picture of Amata as bacchant recalls Dido in a similar situation (e.g., 4. 300-1). Dido preparing for death, *sanguineam volvens aciem* (4. 643) anticipates Amata *sanguineam torquens aciem* (7. 399).

118 Cf. also 4. 586-87.

119 And her death is defined as *cladem* at 604.

120 On Virgil's originality here while reworking Lucretius, see Austin's splendid note.

121 For further detail, see Putnam (1998), 97-118.

122 *Poenorum in arvis* (12. 4) find its echo in the *puniceae pennae* (12. 750) that frighten the stag.

123 This is the only occasion in the epic where he is compared to an animal, one on one. At 2. 355-58 he is one of group of wolves.

124 Though people are named in the first lines of other books (Turnus himself, e.g., in book 9), in no other book does a particular character receive the first word.

125 9. 792-96.

126 See Hardie's note on 9. 342, illustrating how Virgil carefully orchestrates a double comparison there with both Euryalus and Nisus.

127 Turnus is also associated with forms of fury at 9. 691 and 760; 11. 486 and 901; 12. 101. Aeneas is given, or subjected, to fury at 10. 545 and 802; 12. 946.

128 It is often said that Turnus deserves death for breaking the treaty that he asks for here. The treaty is in fact broken by the augur Tolumnius at the instigation of Juturna (see especially lines 220 and 244). Turnus only returns to battle after the wounding of Aeneas by an unknown assailant (324). See note 155 and further discussion in the Epilogue, pp. 121-22. Those who consider him irreligious (e.g., as a "rebel against the gods" [Stahl (1990), 177]) might reconsider moments such as *Aen* 9. 1-24 and 12. 219-21.

129 The pronominal adjective varies according to whether the line is being translated from book 4 or book 12.

130 Lines 882-83 in Juturna's speech (*...aut quicquam mihi dulce meorum / te sine,*

frater, erit? ["...or will anything of mine be sweet to me without you, brother?"])
also have resonances, now forward as well as backward.

Anna's words remind us of Dido addressing Aeneas at 4. 317-18: *si bene quid de te merui, fuit aut tibi quicquam / dulce meum* ("If I deserved anything good from you, or if anything of mine was sweet to you"). They also anticipate a more imminent passage that we will examine later (12. 947-48): *...tune hinc spoliis indute meorum / eripiare mihi'* ("Are you, clothed in the spoils of what is mine, to be snatched from me?").

131   To the several parallels that we have discussed between Turnus and Dido we might add the similarities of their deaths as reflected in the final hexameters of books 4. 704-5 : *...omnis et una / dilapsus calor atque in ventos vita recessit* ("...and with it all warmth left her, and her life departed into the winds") (Williams (1972)) and 12. 952: *...vitaque cum gemitu fugit indignata sub umbras* ("...and with a groan his life flees, resentful, under the shades"). Though other books end with deaths, none has language that corresponds to the reverberation of *in ventos vita* in *vita...sub umbras*.

132   See Thomas (1998), *passim*.

133   The step from Jupiter, described by the narrator as *saevi regis* (12. 849) as he unleashes the Dira, to Aeneas at the epic's end, wielding his spear that brings *exitium dirum* (12. 924), is not large.

134   *De Rerum Natura* 4. 173.

135   We think ahead also to 951: *illi solvuntur frigore membra.*

136   On the two other occasions where Virgil uses the phrase *gelidus sanguis* (*Aen.* 3. 30 and 259), it is glossed by the word *formidine.*

137   It is well to remember here that the only other occasion on which Virgil uses the past participle of *accendo* with *furiis* is in book 7 (392), of the mothers maddened by the Fury Allecto.

138   There is a virtuoso parody of lines 903-4 by Martial (3. 44. 10-11).

139   The life of Turnus is of course still fleeing as the epic ends (*fugit*, 12. 952).

140   The phrase appears in prose only at Pliny *epi.* 7. 25. 4.

141   *Th.* 11. 548 for the first, *Th.* 11. 517 for the second.

142   *M.* 11. 326 and *Th.* 11. 601-2.

143   For *quies* as the sleep of death, see commentators on Lucretius *DRN* 3. 211 and on *Aen.* 10. 745. In the case of Turnus, it is *quies* itself, powerfully personified, whom we anticipate fulfilling the role that Euryalus's mother cannot assume in book 9.

144   Most critics (e.g., Munro, Bailey, Ernout and Robin, Leonard and Smith, Kenney with skepticism) imagine Lucretius as imitating Sappho 2, and perhaps even Catullus's rendition of her in poem 51. There may be a secondary element of eroticism in Virgil's simile. If so, there would be strong irony in attributing the parallels to Turnus here.

145   Not that these lines as well lack novelties, e.g., the unusual use of *sonere* for the expected *sonare.*

146   *Aen.* 9. 446-49, 10. 507.

147   *Aen.* 7. 57.

148   *TD* 4. 21.

149   Just as Shakespeare skirts any full explanation of Iago's deep hatred of Othello,

so Virgil never directly defines the reasons for the *odia* that Turnus perceives in Aeneas's behavior.

150 The word *dirum* recalls the presence of the *Dira* at 845, 869, and 914. Especially given the connection with Jupiter, an ancient reader would have duly pondered the etymology of *dira* as *dei ira*. See Maltby, s.v. *dirum*, and O'Hara (1996), 240.

151 The phrase *volat atri turbinis instar* (12. 923), applied to Aeneas's spear, is also a careful reminder of how Virgil describes Aeneas himself in fury at the end of his rampage in book 10 (602-4):

> talia per campos edebat funera ductor
> Dardanius torrentis aquae vel turbinis atri
> more furens.

> Such deaths the Trojan leader dealt through the fields as he raged like a torrent of water or a black whirlwind.

The verbal parallels form one of several links between the moment in book 10 where Aeneas goes wild in the wake of Pallas's death and the poem's conclusion. As the final chapter shows in detail, Turnus is the last in the series of such victims.

152 In having us look closely at Aeneas's *telum* (12. 919), Virgil asks that we remember Anchises's command to the ghost of Julius Caesar: *proice tela manu, sanguis meus!* (Without weapons one cannot resort to the physical violence by which vengeance is extracted.) Aeneas's deadly *tela*, to be used metaphorically against Dido, are already present at 4. 149.

153 For a survey of recent criticism on the end of the *Aeneid*, see Hardie (1998), 99-101, and Fratantuono, 402, n. 22 and 25.

154 Once the hesitations of the golden bough and Vulcan are past, we can anticipate the initiation and crafting of Roman history. Once Aeneas's concluding hesitation is over, we launch a pattern for the severity of individual heroism into that history.

155 A common defense of Aeneas's action rests on the notion that Turnus is a treaty-breaker, and therefore deserves to be killed. But nothing in Virgil's language in the last eighty lines of the poem makes any reference to the treaty's rupture, which, in any case, is an event in which Turnus had no part. It is also often said that Turnus must die because his death is an example of *devotio*, the offering of his life for his army by its chief. Again, Virgil's text offers no evidence for such a theory; moreover, such an act of self-sacrifice must be willing, whereas Turnus prays for life, not death.

156 *Iram* (4), *irae* (11), *irarum* (25). See also 130 (*irae*).

157 For Turnus and Jupiter's Fury, cf. 12. 867: *illi membra novus solvit formidine torpor* (But a new numbness slackens his limbs with fear). For Turnus's fear at the end, see *timentem* (875), *terrent* (bis, 894-95), *metu*, *tremescit* (916). For Trojan fear in book 1, see *timor* (450), *metum* (562).

158 See above, ch. 3, n. 94.

159 Berres (18) speaks of the phrase as a "Formulierung" without mentioning that it is Virgil's only example of the triple conjunction.

160 In book 2, Virgil makes the point specific at 576 (*ulcisci*) and 587 (*ultricis*).

161 We should also note Virgil's use of the word *exuviae* to describe both "remnants" left to Dido by Aeneas (4. 496, 507, 651) and the baldric of Pallas, now the spoils of Turnus but also a reminder for Aeneas (12. 946).

162 At Pallas's moment of departure we are told of Evander that "his servants carried him in a faint inside the palace" (*famuli conlapsum in tecta ferebant*, 8. 584). We recall what happens to Dido after her exchanges with Aeneas (4. 391 92): *...suscipiunt famulae conlapsaque membra / marmoreo referunt thalamo stratisque reponunt* (Her servants raise her up and carry her fainting limbs to her marble chamber and place her on her bed). The remembrance fosters a parallel between Evander's emotional reaction to his son and Dido's to her lover, Aeneas.

163 11. 68-71. Cf. the parallel comparison of the dead Euryalus at 9. 435-37. For *levi... pectore*, see *levia pectora* of Amata and her comrades (7. 349). For *niveus*, cf. *Aen.* 8. 387 (Venus's *niveis lacertis*) and Catullus 64. 384, on Polyxena's beauty in death (*niveos...virginis artus*).

164 Line 11. 75 telling of how Dido interspersed her weaving with gold is an exact repetition of 4. 262 describing a mantle Aeneas wears which she also had made.

165 Of more than a dozen translations of the passage into English that I have consulted, only Dryden nears Virgil's exact wording: "His left young Pallas kept, fix'd to his side." St. Augustine (*Confessions* 8.16.27) uses the phrase *affixus lateri meo* of his friend Alypius as both are in the throes of preparation for conversion. The rich implications of the reference, which I owe to Stephen van Beek, deserve separate treatment.

166 See 4. 77-79 and the narration that follows.

167 9. 578-79, where I accept Housman's emendation of *lateri manus* to *alte lateri*. This would not change *infixa* and *lateri* in any case. See Williams (1973)and Hardie (1994) ad loc. For forms of *figo* and its compounds in similar settings, see *Aen.* 4. 4, 70 and 689; 12. 7.

168 Tibullus 1. 5. 61-62.

169 This is the meaning of *meorum* at *Aen.* 4. 342-43 (*dulcis...meorum / reliquias*).

170 The reader should compare Aeneas's use of *mihi* at 11. 97 in his brief farewell to Pallas, an ethical dative usually either omitted in translations and commentaries or not given its full force. As Williams (1973) notes ad loc, the language deliberately recalls Achilles's final farewell to Patroclus (*Iliad* 23. 19). There Homer's μοι is equally important and equally hard to render into English. The immediately subsequent apostrophe (*maxime Palla*) is noticeable for its hyperbole. Aeneas has known the youth for only a few days.

171 It is of course deeply ironic that the final expression of immediate emotional feeling on the part of Aeneas is directly at odds with the formulation of ethical values asked of him by his father when he addresses him as model Roman.

172 Virgil makes no attempt to soothe his reader's response to Aeneas's rage by dwelling on some vague notion that it was his duty to kill the leader of his opposition, especially one who took advantage of his wounding to attempt to sway the battle. It bears repeating here that not only does Turnus not break the treaty, he is not even listed by Virgil among those who take immediate advantage of a return to hostilities (see 12. 266-310).

I do not mean to imply that Virgil condems negative emotionality outright.

For instance, an augur can speak of the *iustus dolor* (7. 500-1) and *merita ira* (501, confirmed by the narrator at 10. 714 as *iustae irae*) of his people against Mezentius.

173 By comparison with Homer, Virgil raises the moral stakes at the end because Turnus, unlike Hector, the prey of Achilles's inexorable pursuit, could remain alive, should Aeneas so decide at the end. It is not now a question of pleading by father to ransom the body of his son for proper burial but of a publicly vanquished hero asking for his life.

174 I have not commented on what ancient philosophers, if any, Virgil might have us call to our aid for help in evaluating the morality of Aeneas's final action. I agree with Hardie (1998), p. 100: "...those who seek a philosophical solution run the risk of simply exporting the problem of interpreting the end of the *Aeneid* into an unresolved dispute between ancient philosophical schools." Appeal especially to Aristotle NE 4. 5 (1125b31-1126a2)] is unfruitful. According to Aristotle, anger is justified, but only when displayed by someone who is good-tempered and not led by emotion "but as principle [logos] may ordain...since the gentle-tempered man is not prompt to seek redress for injuries, but rather inclined to forgive them" (Rackham). One is hard-pressed to describe fury-driven, vengeful, unforgiving Aeneas as in any way good-tempered, according to Aristotle's definition. See further discussion in the Epilogue, pp. 123-24.

175 Harriet Beecher Stowe (1811-1898) published *Uncle Tom's Cabin* serially in 1851 and in book form the following year. Samuel Langhorne Clemens (Mark Twain) (1835-1910) began writing *Huckleberry Finn* in 1876 and published the novel in 1884.

176 Lucius Caecilius Firmianus Lactantius (c. 240-c. 320 CE). The *Divinae Institutiones* was written between 303 and 311.

177 Maurus (or Marius) Honoratus Servius, late fourth-early fifth century CE. He is famous as an interlocutor in Macrobius's *Saturnalia*, whose dramatic date is probably 383 CE, where he is introduced as a young man. For details, see Ziolkowski and Putnam, 628-36.

178 Adams (1767-1848), distinguished lawyer and professor, was the sixth president of the United States of America.

179 Grimké (1786-1834), attorney, author, and social activist, was a state senator from South Carolina.

180 Even though I propose several parallels among the works of the three authors, I make no claim, here and in what follows, that Harriet Beecher Stowe and Mark Twain were thinking specifically of the *Aeneid* and its conclusion as they wrote their climactic pages. My purpose is to use the two nineteenth-century texts as help in elucidating the moral dimensions of the *Aeneid*'s ending by suggesting similarities in the ethical background of the three masterpieces.

181 Or "with them while they were still alive."

182 Lactantius *The Divine Institutes, Books I-VII*, trans. M. F. McDonald (Washington, 1964), modified and emended.

183 It is actually Tolumnius the augur who hurls the first weapon (12. 266).

184 The other accusation regularly made by critics against Turnus, that he was prone to *violentia* (as Virgil himself notes at *Aen.* 11. 376 and 12. 9, 45; cf. 10. 151, 11. 354), collapses in the face of Aeneas's conduct in book 10.

185 Adams, 244-45.

186 Cf. also Aristotle *Rhetorica* 1. 10. 1368. 11-14 on the difference between acts of revenge, which are caused by passion and anger, and of punishment. To paraphrase: the latter is inflicted in the interest of the sufferer, the former in the interest of him who inflicts it so that he may gain satisfaction.

187 Grimké (1835), p. 16.

188 Grimké (1830), p. 20

189 Grimké (1834), p. 22. I can't resist a final flourish, drawn from Grimké (1830), p. 71, note L: "I would rather know by heart, Campbell's lovely and spotless poem, Gertrude of Wyoming, than the 4th Book of the Aeneid...."

190 Among other contemporary works I think of Nathaniel Hawthorne's *The Scarlet Letter* (1850), Herman Melville's *Moby Dick* and Hawthorne's *The House of the Seven Gables* (both 1851), Henry David Thoreau's *Walden* (1854), and Walt Whitman's *Leaves of Grass* (1855).

191 It might be mentioned here that Harriet Beecher Stowe read Virgil from the age of thirteen (1824), when she entered her sister Catherine's school in Hartford, Connecticut, and taught him beginning in 1827. At the start of chapter XXX of *Uncle Tom's Cabin* she quotes in Latin, and slightly varies, *Aen*. 3. 658 in a comparison describing a slave warehouse in New Orleans.

192 Stowe, p. 578. I follow the text as printed in the Penguin American Library edition.

193 Stowe, p. 582.

194 Stowe, p. 582-83.

195 It is fair to say, however, that the helplessness of the slave, confronting his owner's concentrated savagery, is merely more apparent now than ever. Turnus's vulnerability, however, has developed only over the course of the *Aeneid's* last book, as we move from initial, metaphoric wound to the final death-blow.

196 *Uncle Tom's Cabin* follows the *Odyssey* as well as the *Iliad* in having at least some respite from previous violence and, in the case of the former, in some ways even a happy ending. In Stowe's novel, the two hiding slaves, Cassy and Emmeline, escape to join Eliza, George, and Harry in Canada. After watching Tom die, George Shelby renounces slavery and frees his slaves. Virgil leaves us only with the meaning of a ferocious killing to ponder.

197 Twain, 211-14.

198 It is worth remembering here that Virgil uses a form of the word *oculus* four times in the last thirty lines of his poem (*Aen*. 12. 920, 930, 939, 945) and a form of the word *lumen* once (935).

199 We learn shortly later that at her death Miss Watson has in fact granted freedom to Jim in her will.

200 For an appraisal of the interconnection between the poem and Augustus's early *curriculum vitae*, see Putnam (2002), *passim*.

201 Putnam (1965), ix.

202 Austin (1967), pp. 280-81.

203 5.5.8; 7.63.5.

204 Heinze, Lyne (1987), Hardie (1997a).

205 See also Putnam (2006).

206 Thomas (2001), Putnam (2004).

207 The most striking example is *King Lear*.

208 Steiner, Nuttall.

209 Dodds, p. 68.

210 "which, what concerned him most, would encompass at one and the same time the origins of the city of Rome and of Augustus," *VSD* 21.

211 *B* 6.3-5; *VSD* 31.

212 To which attest the numerous graffiti on the walls of Pompeii.

213 Den Hengst, pp. 160-76.

214 Schmidt.

215 Thomas (2001), pp. 25-54.

216 Herrnstein Smith.

217 Stahl (1990).

218 For comparison with epic predecessors and successors of Vergil in this respect, see Putnam (1998), pp. 91-94.

219 Zanker.

220 6. 450-74. The mathematical center would be the transition between book 6 and book 7. Although this passage is marked as well, book 6 clearly is the centerpiece of the epic, and as such its center carries a heavy emphasis. For arguments and further suggested connections of the ending with the center of the *Aeneid*, see Putnam (2010).

221 It has even been ingeniously shown that in fact Turnus and Dido are relatives, stemming from the line of Inachus, the first through Belus, the latter through Agenor, in Schmitzer.

222 Putnam (2010), pp. 20-22.

223 Hardie (1997b), pp. 150-51.

224 It is tempting to see Horace *Odes* 1.37 in this light also.

225 Hardie (1986), 125-42.

226 Seminal is Hardie (1993), pp. 19-35. For a recent treatment, see Panoussi (2010), 52-65.

227 *Poetica* 1452a.

228 The analysis of tragic reversal as a key element in Sophocles' *Oedipus Tyrannus* by Vernant, from which the following examples are taken, provides striking parallels with Vergil's treatment. See also Knox (1957).

229 Andreae. He does not acknowledge Dante as an implicit predecessor in this interpretation, cf. *Inferno* 26.59-60.

230 Quoted by Wiseman, p. 124.

231 Bandera, Hardie (1993).

232 Again, Vernant's analysis of Oedipus as scapegoat provides a striking parallel.

233 Panoussi (2010).

234 Toll. See also a very convincing but little-read (because presented in Dutch) argument in Schrijvers.

235 Bandera, p. 233; Hardie (1983), pp. 22-23.

236 "All were anxious as to who would lead them," Enn. *frg.* 78 Skutsch; this parallel and the following adduced by Hardie, *loc. cit.*

237 Hardie (1997a), with literature.

238 For some of these and other answers to this question, see Hardie (1997a).

239 Beacham.

240   The term is Stephen Harrison's, from his study of the same title (*Generic Enrichment in Vergil and Horace* [Oxford 2007]).

241   This idea is strikingly corroborated in the preface to *de oratoribus veteribus* of Dionysius of Halicarnassus, for which see Hidber. I thank Casper de Jonge for this reference.

242   Wiseman.

Bibliography

Adams, John Quincy, *Lectures on Rhetoric and Oratory* (Cambridge, 1810; repr. Delmar, 1997).

Ahl, F., trans., *Virgil: Aeneid*, (New York, 2007).

Anderson, W. S., "Vergil's Second *Iliad*," *TAPA* 88 (1957), 17–30; repr. in Hardie (1999), III, 74–86.

—, "Pastor Aeneas: On Pastoral Themes in the *Aeneid*," *TAPA* 99 (1968), 1–17.

Andreae, B. *Laokoon und die Gründung Roms* (Mainz, 1988).

Austin, R. G., "*Aeneid* 2. 567–588," *CQ* 11 (1961), 185–98.

—, ed., *P. Vergili Maronis Aeneidos: Liber Secundus* (Oxford, 1964).

—, [untitled review], *JRS* 57 (1967), 280–81.

Bailey, C., ed. and trans., *Titi Lucreti Cari: De Rerum Natura, Libri Sex*, 3 vol. (Oxford, 1947).

Bandera, C. "Sacrificial Levels in Virgil's *Aeneid*," *Arethusa* 14 (1981), 217–39.

Barchiesi, A., "Il lamento di Giuturna," *MD* 1 (1978), 99–121.

—, "Rappresentazioni del dolore e interpretatione nell'Eneide," *Antike und Abendland* 40 (1994), 109–24; trans. as "Representations of Suffering and Interpretation in the *Aeneid*," in Hardie (1999), III, 324–44.

Beacham, R. "The Emperor as Impresario: Producing the Pageantry of Power," in Galinsky, K., ed., *The Cambridge Companion to the Age of Augustus* (Cambridge, 2005), 151–74.

Berno, F. R., "Un *truncus*, molti re: Priamo, Agamemnone, Pompeo (Virgilio, Seneca, Lucano)," *Maia* 56 (2004), 79–84.

Berres, T., *Vergil und die Helenaszene* (Heidelberg, 1992).

Bowie, A., "The Death of Priam: Allegory and History in the *Aeneid*," *CQ* 40 (1990), 470–81.

Boyle, A., *The Chaonian Dove: Studies in the* Eclogues, Georgics, *and* Aeneid. Mnemosyne Supplement 95 (Leiden, 1986).

Braund, S., and C. Gill, eds., *The Passions in Roman Thought and Literature* (Chicago, 1997).

— and G. Most, eds., *Ancient Anger: Perspectives from Homer to Galen* (Cambridge, 2003).

Brooks, R. A., "Discolor Aura: Reflections on the Golden Bough," *AJP* 74 (1953), 260–80, reprinted in *Virgil: A Collection of Critical Essays*, ed. S. Commager (Englewood Cliffs, 1966), 143–63.

Burke, P. F., Jr., "Mezentius and the First-Fruits," *Vergilius* 20 (1974), 28–29.

Camps, W. A., *An Introduction to Virgil's* Aeneid (Oxford, 1969).

Chew, K., "*Inscius pastor*: Ignorance and Aeneas' Identity in the *Aeneid*," *Latomus* 61 (2002), 616–27.

Clausen, W. V., "An Interpretation of the *Aeneid*," *HSCP* 68 (1964), 139–47.

Connolly, J., "Figuring the Founder: Vergil and the Challenge of Autocracy," in Farrell and Putnam (2010), 404–17.

Conte, G. B., *The Poetry of Pathos*: *Studies in Virgilian Epic* (Oxford, 2007).

Day Lewis, C., trans., *The Aeneid of Virgil* (Garden City, 1953).

de la Cerda, J. L., *P. Virgilii Maronis*: *Priores sex libri Aeneidos* (Lyons, 1612).

Den Hengst, D., *Emperors and Historiography* (Leiden, 2010).

Dillon, S., and K. Welch, eds., *Representations of War in Ancient Rome* (Cambridge, 2006).

Dodds, E. R., "On Misunderstanding the *Oedipus Rex*," in E. R. Dodds, *The Ancient Concept of Progress and Other Essays on Greek Literature and Belief* (Oxford, 1973).

Duckworth, G. E., "Turnus as a Tragic Character," *Vergilius* 4 (1940), 5–17.

Dyson, J., *King of the Wood* (Norman, 2001).

Ernout, A., and L. Robin, edd., *Lucrèce, De rerum natura*, 3 vol. (Paris, 1962).

Fagles, R., *Virgil*: *The Aeneid* (New York, 2006).

Fairclough, H. R., trans., *Virgil*. Rev. by G. P. Goold. 2 vols. Vol. 1: *Ecolgues, Georgics, Aeneid I–VI* (Cambridge and London, 1999). Vol. 2: *Aeneid VII–XII, Appendix Vergiliana* (Cambridge and London, 2000).

Farrell, J., and M. C. J. Putnam, eds., *A Companion to Vergil's* Aeneid *and Its Tradition* (Malden and Oxford, 2010).

Feeney, D., "The Reconciliations of Juno," *CQ* 34 (1984), 179–94; repr. in S. J. Harrison, ed., *Oxford Readings in Vergil's* Aeneid (Oxford, 1990), 339–62, and in Hardie (1999), IV, 392–413.

Fish, J., "Anger, Philodemus's Good King, and the Helen Episode of the *Aeneid*," in D. Armstrong, J. Fish, P. Johnston, and M. Skinner, eds., *Vergil, Philodemus, and the Augustans* (Austin, 2004), 111–38.

Fitzgerald, J., ed., *Passions and Moral Progress in Greco-Roman Thought* (London, 2008).

Fratantuono, L., *Madness Unchained*: *A Reading of Virgil's* Aeneid (Lanham, 2007).

Galinsky, G. K., "The Anger of Aeneas," *AJP* 109 (1988), 321–48; repr. in Hardie (1999), IV, 434–57.

Gill, C., *The Structured Self in Hellenistic and Roman Thought* (Oxford, 2006).

—, "Reactive and Objective Attitudes: Anger in Virgil's *Aeneid* and Hellenistic Philosophy," in Braund and Most (2003), 208–28.

Gransden, K. W., *Virgil's Iliad*: *An Essay on Epic Narrative* (Cambridge, 1984).

Grimké, Thomas Smith, *Oration on the Advantages, to Be Derived from the Introduction of the Bible, and of Sacred Literature, as Essential Parts of All Education...Delivered before the Connecticut Alpha of the P[hi] B[eta] K[appa] Society, Sept. 7, 1830* (New Haven, 1830).

—, *Oration on the Comparative Elements and Dutys of Grecian and American Eloquence* (Cincinnati, 1834).

—, *Oration on American Education: Delivered before the Western Literary Institute and College of Professional Teachers, at their Fourth Annual Meeting, October, 1834* (Cincinnati, 1835).

Gross, N. P., "Mantles Woven with Gold: Pallas' Shroud and the End of the *Aeneid*," *CJ* 99 (2003–4), 135–56.

Hardie, P. R., *Virgil's* Aeneid: *Cosmos and Imperium* (Oxford, 1986).

—, *The Epic Successors of Virgil* (Cambridge, 1993).

—, ed., *Virgil: Aeneid, Book IX* (Cambridge, 1994).

—, "Vergil and Tragedy," in C. Martindale, ed., *The Cambridge Companion to Vergil* (Cambridge, 1997a).

—, "Closure in Latin Epic," in D. H. Roberts, F. M. Dunn, and D. Fowler, eds., *Classical Closure: Reading the End in Greek and Latin Literature* (Princeton, 1997b), 139–62.

—, *Virgil. Greece and Rome.* New Surveys in the Classics #28 (Oxford, 1998).

—, ed., *Virgil: Critical Assessments of Classical Authors* (London and New York, 1999), vols. I–IV.

Harris, W., *Restraining Rage: The Ideology of Anger Control in Classical Antiquity* (Cambridge, 2001).

Harrison, S. J., "Virgil as a Poet of War," *PVS* 19 (1988), 48–68.

—, ed., *Vergil: Aeneid 10* (Oxford, 1991).

Hedges, C., *War Is a Force That Gives Us Meaning* (New York, 2002).

Heinze, R., *Virgils epische Technik* (Leipzig, 1928); trans. as *Virgil's Epic Technique*, by H. Harvey, D. Harvey, and F. Robertson (Berkeley, 1993).

Herrnstein Smith, B. *Poetic Closure: A Study of How Poems End* (Chicago, 1968).

Hidber, T. *Das klassizistische Manifest des Dionys von Halikarnass: Die Praefatio zu De Oratoribus Veteribus* (Stuttgart, 1996).

Hölscher, T., "The Transformation of Victory into Power: From Event to Structure," in Dillon and Welch (2006), 27–48.

Hope, V. M, "Trophies and Tombstones: Commemorating the Roman Soldier," *World Archaeology* 35 (2003), 79–97.

Hornsby, R. A., "The Armor of the Slain," *PhQ* 45 (1966), 347–59.

—, "The Pastor in the Poetry of Vergil," *CJ* 63 (1968), 145–52.

Horsfall, N. M., ed., *A Companion to the Study of Virgil* (Leiden, 1995).

—, ed., *Virgil, Aeneid 2: A Commentary* (Leiden, 2008).

Housman, A. E., ed., *M. Manilius: Astronomicon* (Cambridge, 1937).

James, H., *Shakespeare's Troy: Drama, Politics, and the Translation of Empire* (Cambridge, 1997).

James, S. L., "Establishing Rome with the Sword: *Condere* in the *Aeneid*," *AJP* 116 (1995), 623–37.

Johnson, W. R., *Darkness Visible: A Study of Vergil's* Aeneid (Berkeley, 1976).

Kallendorf, C., *The Other Virgil: "Pessimistic" Readings of the* Aeneid *in Early Modern Culture* (Oxford, 2007).

Kaster, R., *Emotion, Restraint, and Community in Ancient Rome* (Oxford, 2005).

Kenney, E. J., ed. *Titus Lucretius Carus: De rerum natura: Book 3* (Cambridge, 1984).

Kerrigan, J., *Revenge Tragedy: Aeschylus to Armageddon* (Oxford, 1996).

Knauer, G. N., *Die Aeneis und Homer: Studien zur poetischen Technik Vergils mit Listen der Homerzitate in der Aeneis.* Hypomnemata 7 (Göttingen, 1964).

Knox, B., *Oedipus at Thebes: Sophocles' Tragic Hero and His Time* (New Haven, 1957).

Knox, P. E., "Savagery in the *Aeneid* and Virgil's Ancient Commentators," *CJ* 92 (1997), 225–33.

Lattimore, R., trans., *Homer: The Iliad* (Chicago, 1962).

Leonard, W. R., and S. B. Smith, edd., *T. Lucreti Cari: De Rerum Natura, Libri Sex* (Madison, 1942).

Levitan, W. "'Give Up the Beginning?': Juno's Mindful Wrath (*Aeneid* 1.370)," *LCM* 18 (1993), 14.

Lombardo, S., trans. *Virgil: Aeneid* (Indianapolis, 2005).

Lowrie, M., "Vergil and Founding Violence," *Cardozo Law Review* 24 (2005), 945–76; repr. in Farrell and Putnam (2010), 391–403.

Lyne, R. O. A. M., "Virgil and the Politics of War," CQ 33 (1983a), 188–203; repr. in R. O. A. M. Lyne, *Collected Papers on Latin Poetry* (Oxford, 2007), 115–35.

—, "Lavinia's Blush: Vergil, *Aeneid* 12. 64–70," *Greece and Rome* 30 (1983b), 55–64; repr. in R. O. A. M. Lyne, *Collected Papers on Latin Poetry* (Oxford, 2007), 136–43.

—, *Further Voices in Vergil's Aeneid* (Oxford, 1987).

—, *Words and the Poet*: *Characteristic Techniques of Style in the Aeneid* (Oxford, 1989).

MacKay, L. A., "Achilles as Model for Aeneas," TAPA 88 (1957), 11–16; repr. in Hardie (1999), III, 87–92.

—, "Hero and Theme in the *Aeneid*," TAPA 94 (1963), 157–66.

Maltby, R. *A Lexicon of Ancient Latin Etymologies*. Arca 25 (Leeds, 1991).

Mandelbaum, A., trans., *The Aeneid of Virgil*, (New York, 1981).

McWilliams, J. P., Jr., *The American Epic*: *Transforming a Genre, 1770–1860* (Cambridge, 1989).

Morgan, G., "Dido the Wounded Deer," *Vergilius* 40 (1994), 67–68.

Munro, H. A. J., ed. and trans., *T. Lucretius Carus: De Rerum Natura, Libri Sex*, 3 vol. (Cambridge, 1886).

Nethercut, W. R., "Invasion in the *Aeneid*," G&R 15 (1968), 82–95.

Nielson, K. P., "The *Tropaion* in the *Aeneid*," *Vergilius* 29 (1983), 27–33.

Nuttall, A. D. *Why Does Tragedy Give Pleasure?* (Oxford, 1996).

O'Hara, J., *True Names*: *Virgil and the Alexandrian Tradition of Etymological Wordplay* (Ann Arbor, 1996).

Oliensis, E., *Freud's Rome*: *Psycholanalysis and Latin Poetry* (Cambridge, 2009).

O'Sullivan, T., "Death *ante ora parentum* in Virgil's *Aeneid*," TAPA 139 (2009), 447–86.

Panoussi, V. *Greek Tragedy in Vergil's* "Aeneid": *Ritual, Empire, and Intertext* (Cambridge, 2009).

—, "Aeneas' Sacral Authority," in Farrell and Putnam (2010), 52–65.

Parry A., "The Two Voices of Virgil's *Aeneid*," *Arion* 2 (1963), 66–80; repr. in Hardie (1999), III, 49–64.

Pascal, C. B., "The Dubious Devotion of Turnus," TAPA 120 (1990), 251–68.

Pease, A. S., ed., *Publi Vergili Maronis Aeneidos*: *Liber Quartus* (Cambridge, 1935; reprint Darmstadt, 1963).

Perkell, C., "The Lament of Juturna: Pathos and Interpretation in the *Aeneid*," TAPA 127 (1997), 257–86.

Petter, G. J., "Desecration and Expiation in the *Aeneid*," *Vergilius* 40 (1994), 76–84.

Pöschl, V., *Die Dichtkunst Virgils*: *Bild und Symbol in der Aeneis* (Innsbruck, 1950); trans. by G. Seligson as *The Art of Vergil*: *Image and Symbol in the* Aeneid (Ann Arbor, 1962).

Polleichtner, W., *Emotional Questions*: *Vergil, the Emotions, and the Transformation of Epic Poetry*. Bochumer Altertumswissenschaftliches Colloquium #82 (Trier, 2009).

Powell, A., *Virgil the Partisan: A Study in the Re-Integration of Classics* (Swansea, 2008).

Putnam, M. C. J., *The Poetry of the* Aeneid (Cambridge, 1965; repr. Ithaca, 1988).

—, "*Pius* Aeneas and the Metamorphosis of Lausus," *Arethusa* 14 (1981), 139–56; repr. in H. Bloom, ed., *Modern Critical Views: Virgil* (New York, 1986), 157–71.

—, "The Hesitation of Aeneas," *Atti del Convegno mondiale scientifico di studi su Virgilio 1981* (Milan, 1984), 233–52; repr. in Hardie (1999), IV, 414–33.

—, "Possessiveness, Sexuality and Heroism in the *Aeneid*," *Vergilius* 31 (1985), 1–21.

—, "Anger, Blindness and Insight in Virgil's *Aeneid*," *Apeiron* 23 (1990), 7–40.

—, *Virgil's Aeneid: Interpretation and Influence* (Chapel Hill, 1995).

—, *Virgil's Epic Designs* (New Haven, 1998).

—, "*Aeneid* 12: Unity in Closure," in C. Perkell, ed., *Reading Vergil's* Aeneid: *An Interpretative Guide* (Norman, 1999), 210–30.

—, "Vergil's *Aeneid*: The Final Lines," in Spence (2001), 86–104.

—, "Vergil's *Aeneid* and the Evolution of Augustus," in W. S. Anderson and L. Quartarone, eds., *Approaches to Teaching Vergil's* Aeneid (New York, 2002), 14–22.

—, ed., *Maffeo Vegio: Short Epics*. Edited and translated by Michael C. J. Putnam (Cambridge, MA, 2004).

—, "Vergil's *Aeneid*," in J. M. Foley, ed., *A Companion to Ancient Epic* (Malden and Oxford, 2005), 452–75.

—, "The *Aeneid* and *Paradise Lost*: Ends and Conclusions," *Literary Imagination* 8 (2006), 387–410.

—, "Some Virgilian Unities," in P. Hardie and H. Moore, eds., *Classical Literary Careers and Their Reception* (Cambridge, 2010), 17–38.

Rackham, H., ed. and trans, *Aristotle: The Nicomachean Ethics* (Cambridge, 1982).

Reed, J. D., *Virgil's Gaze: Nation and Poetry in the* Aeneid (Princeton, 2007).

Reinhold, M., "Vergil in the American Experience from Colonial Times to 1882," in M. Reinhold, *Classica Americana: The Greek and Roman Heritage in the United States* (Detroit, 1984), 221–49.

—, "The Americanization of Aeneas, from Colonial Times to 1882," *Augustan Age* 6 (1987), 207–18.

Richard, C. J., "Vergil and the Early American Republic," in Farrell and Putnam (2010), 355–65.

Rijser, D., *Raphael's Poetics: Ekphrasis, Interaction and Typology in Art and Poetry of High Renaissance Rome* (Amsterdam, 2006).

Schmidt, E. A., "The Meaning of Vergil's *Aeneid*: American and German Approaches," *CW* 94 (2001), 145–71.

Schmitzer, U., "Turnus und die Danaiden: Mythologische Verstrickung und personale Verantwortung," *GB* 20 (1994) 109–126.

Schrijvers, P. H., "Een oud verhaal," *Lampas* 28 (1995), 121–135.

Serpa, F., *Il Punto su Virgilio* (Bari, 1987).

Shankman, S., *In Search of the Classic: Reconsidering the Greco-Roman Tradition, Homer to Valéry and Beyond* (University Park, 1994).

Skutsch, O., ed., *The Annals of Quintus Ennius* (Oxford, 1985).

Smolenaars, H., "Hector's Death and Augustan Politics," in J. Bremmer, T. van den Hout, and R. Peters, eds., *Hidden Futures: Death and Immortality in Ancient Egypt, Anatolia, the Classical, Biblical and Arabic-Islamic World* (Amsterdam, 1994), 125–51.

Spence, S., ed., *Poets and Critics Read Virgil* (New Haven, 2001).

Stahl, H.-P., "The Death of Turnus," in K. Raaflaub and M. Toher, eds., *Between Republic and Empire: Interpretations of Augustus and His Principate* (Berkeley, 1990), 174–211.

—, ed., *Vergil's* Aeneid: *Augustan Epic and Political Context* (London, 1998).

Steiner, G., *The Death of Tragedy* (London, 1961).

Stowe, Harriet Beecher, *Uncle Tom's Cabin*. Penguin American Library (New York, 1981).

Tarrant, R., "The Last Book of the *Aeneid*," *Syllecta Classica* 15 (2004), 103–29.

Thomas, R., "The 'Sacrifice' at the End of the *Georgics*, Aristaeus, and Vergilian Closure," *CP* 86 (1991), 211–18.

—, "The Isolation of Turnus: *Aeneid* Book 12," in Stahl (1998), 271–302

—, *Virgil and the Augustan Reception* (Cambridge, 2001).

Toll, K. "Making Roman-Ness and the 'Aeneid,'" *Classical Antiquity* 16 (1997), 34–56.

Twain, Mark [Samuel L. Clemens], *The Adventures of Huckleberry Finn*. Bantam Classic edition (New York, 2003).

Vernant, J.-P., "Ambiguity and Reversal: On the Enigmatic Structure of *Oedipus Rex*," in E. Segal, ed., *Greek Tragedy: Modern Essays in Criticism* (New York, 1983), 189–209.

Warren, R., "The End of the *Aeneid*," in Spence (2001), 105–17.

West, D. A., "The Deaths of Hector and Turnus," *G&R* 21 (1974), 21–31.

Williams, R. D., ed., *The* Aeneid *of Virgil: Books 1–6* (Basingstoke, 1972).

—, ed., *The* Aeneid *of Virgil: Books 7–12* (Basingstoke, 1973).

Wiseman, T. P. *Remus: A Roman Myth* (Cambridge, 1995).

Zanker, G. *Modes of Viewing in Hellenistic Poetry and Art* (Madison, 2004).

Zarker, J. W., "Amata: Vergil's Other Tragic Queen," *Vergilius* 15 (1969), 2–24.

Ziolkowski, J., and M. C. J. Putnam, eds., *The Virgilian Tradition* (New Haven, 2008).

Bibliographical Handlist of Works on Virgil by Michael C. J. Putnam

BOOKS

The Poetry of the Aeneid (Cambridge, 1965; second printing, 1966; paperback edition, with new preface, Ithaca, 1988).

Virgil's Pastoral Art: Studies in the Eclogues (Princeton, 1970).

Virgil's Poem of the Earth (Princeton, 1979).

Essays on Latin Lyric, Elegy, and Epic (Princeton, 1982).

Virgil's Aeneid: *Interpretation and Influence* (Chapel Hill, 1995).

Virgil's Epic Designs: *Ekphrasis in the* Aeneid (New Haven, 1998).

Maffeo Vegio: *Short Epics*, ed. and trans., with J. Hankins. The I Tatti Renaissance Library #15 (Cambridge, 2004).

Jacopo Sannazaro: *Latin Poetry*, ed. and trans. The I Tatti Renaissance Library #38 (Cambridge, 2009).

Virgil: 2000 Years, *Arethusa* 14:1 (1981), ed., with introduction.

The Virgilian Tradition: The First Fifteen Hundred Years, ed., with J. Ziolkowski (New Haven, 2008).

A Companion to Vergil's Aeneid *and Its Tradition*, ed., with J. Farrell (Malden and Oxford, 2010).

ARTICLES

"Unity and Design in *Aeneid* v," *Harvard Studies in Classical Philology* 66 (1962), 205–39.

"The Riddle of Damoetas," *Mnemosyne* 18 (1965), 150–54.

"*Aeneid* 7 and the *Aeneid*," *American Journal of Philology* 91 (1970), 408–30 (reprinted in P. Hardie, ed., *Virgil: Critical Assessments of Classical Authors* [London, 1999], IV, 244–62).

"The Virgilian Achievement," *Arethusa* 5 (1972), 53–70.

"Italian Virgil and the Idea of Rome," in L. L. Orlin, ed., *Janus: Essays in Ancient and Modern Studies* (Ann Arbor, 1975), 171–199 (reprinted in K. Volk, ed., *Oxford Readings in Classical Studies*: *Vergil's Georgics* [Oxford, 2008], 138–60).

"Virgil's First *Eclogue*: The Rhetoric of Enclosure," *Ramus* 4 (1975), 163–86.

"The Third Book of the *Aeneid*: From Homer to Rome," *Ramus* 9 (1980), 1–21.

"*Pius* Aeneas and the Metamorphosis of Lausus," *Arethusa* 14 (1981), 139–56 (reprinted in H. Bloom, ed., *Modern Critical Views: Virgil* [New York, 1986], 157–71).

"The Hesitation of Aeneas," *Atti del Convegno mondiale scientifico di studi su Virgilio*

1981 (Milano, 1984), 233–52 (reprinted in P. Hardie, ed., *Virgil: Critical Assessments of Classical Authors* [London, 1999], IV: 414–33).

"Romulus Tropaeophorus (*Aeneid* 6. 779–780)," *Classical Quarterly* 35 (1985), 237–40.

"Possessiveness, Sexuality and Heroism in the *Aeneid*," *Vergilius* 31 (1985), 1–21.

"Daedalus, Virgil and the End of Art," *American Journal of Philology* 108 (1987), 173–198 (reprinted in S. Quinn, ed., *Why Vergil? A Collection of Interpretations* [Wauconda, 2000], 220–40).

"Virgil's Inferno," *Materiali e discussioni* 20–21 (1988), 165–202 (reprinted in R. Jacoff and J. Schnapp, eds., *The Poetry of Allusion: Virgil and Ovid in Dante's "Commedia"* [Stanford, 1991], 94–112).

"Virgil and Tacitus *Ann.* 1. 10," *Classical Quarterly* 39 (1989), 563–64.

"Catullus and Virgil, *Aen.* 6. 786–7," *Vergilius* 35 (1989), 28–30.

"Anger, Blindness and Insight in Virgil's *Aeneid*," *Apeiron* 23 (1990), 7–40.

"Virgil's Lapiths," *Classical Quarterly* 40 (1990), 562–66.

"Virgil's Tragic Future: Senecan Drama and the *Aeneid*," in *La Storia, La Letteratura e l'Arte a Roma da Tibero a Domiziano* (Mantua: Accademia Nazionale Virgiliana, 1992), 231–91.

"Umbro, Nireus and Love's Threnody," *Vergilius* 38 (1992), 12–23.

"Virgil's Danaid Ekphrasis," *Illinois Classical Studies* 19 (1994), 171–89.

"Ganymede and Virgilian Ekphrasis," *American Journal of Philology* 116 (1995), 419–40.

"Silvia's Stag and Virgilian Ekphrasis," *Materiali e discussioni* 34 (1995), 107–33.

"Dido and Wine," in O. Murray and M. Tecusan, eds., *In Vino Veritas*. Papers of the British School at Rome (London, 1995), 295–96.

"The Lyric Genius of the *Aeneid*," *Arion* 3 (1995–96), 81–101 (reprinted in S. Quinn, ed., *Why Vergil? A Collection of Interpretations* [Wauconda, 2000], 255–66).

"Dido's Murals and Virgilian Ekphrasis," *Harvard Studies in Classical Philology* 98 (1998), 243–75.

"Turnus, Homer, and Heroism," *Literary Imagination* 1 (1999), 61–78.

"*Aeneid* 12: Unity in Closure," in C. Perkell, ed., *Reading Vergil's* Aeneid: *An Interpretive Guide* (Norman, 1999), 210–30.

"Foreword," in S. Quinn, ed., *Why Vergil? A Collection of Interpretations* (Wauconda, 2000), vii-xii.

"Vergil's *Aeneid*: The Final Lines," in S. Spence, ed., *Poets and Critics Read Vergil* (New Haven, 2001), 86–104.

"The Ambiguity of Art in Virgil's *Aeneid*," *Proceedings of the American Philosophical Society* 145 (2001), 162–83.

"The Loom of Latin," *Transactions of the American Philological Association* 131 (2001), 329–39.

"Ovid, Virgil and Myrrha's Metamorphic Exile," *Vergilius* 47 (2001), 171–93.

"Vergil's *Aeneid* and the Evolution of Augustus," in W. Anderson and L. Quartarone, eds., *Approaches to Teaching Vergil's Aeneid* (New York, 2002), 114–22.

"Turnus' *Phalarica* (*Aen.* IX, 705)," in P. Defosse, ed., *Hommages à Carl Deroux*. Collection Latomus #266 (Brussels, 2002), 433–42.

"Two Ways of Looking at the *Aeneid*," *Classical World* 96 (2003), 177–84.

"Daphne's Roots," *Hermathena* 177/178 (2004–2005), 71–89.

"Virgil and Tibullus 1.1," *Classical Philology* 100 (2005), 123–41.

"Virgil's *Aeneid*," in, J. M. Foley, ed., *A Companion to Ancient Epic* (Malden and Oxford, 2005; paperback, 2009), 452–75.

"The *Aeneid* and *Paradise Lost*: Ends and Conclusions," *Literary Imagination* 8 (2006), 387–410.

"Horace *Carm*. 4. 7 and the Epic Tradition," *Classical World* 100 (2007), 255–62.

"Troy in Latin Literature," *New England Classical Journal* 34 (2007), 195–205.

"Virgil and Wilder's *The Cabala*," *New England Classical Journal* 37 (2010), 113–19.

(with J. Farrell) "Introduction," in J. Farrell and M. C. J. Putnam, eds., *Vergil's* Aeneid *and Its Tradition* (Malden and Oxford, 2010), 1–9.

"Vergil, Ovid, and the Poetry of Exile," in J. Farrell and M. C. J. Putnam, eds., *Vergil's* Aeneid *and its Tradition* (Malden and Oxford, 2010), 80–95.

"Some Virgilian Unities," in P. Hardie and H. Moore, eds., *Classical Literary Careers and Their Reception* (Cambridge, 2010), 17–38.

"Vergil and Seamus Heaney," *Vergilius* 56 (2010), 3–16.

REVIEWS

K. Quinn, *Virgil's* Aeneid: *A Critical Description*, *Vergilius* 14 (1968), 1–3.

F. Demetrio, *Symbols in Comparative Religion and the* Georgics, *Classical World* 62 (1969), 360.

E. Kraggerud, *Aeneisstudien*, *Classical Philology* 64 (1969), 256–57.

L. P. Wilkinson, *The Georgics of Virgil*, *Classical Philology* 65 (1970), 258–59.

W. A. Camps, *An Introduction to Virgil's* Aeneid, *Classical Journal* 66 (1971), 278–80.

R. Hornsby, *Patterns of Action in the* Aeneid, *Classical World* 64 (1971), 204.

K. Galinsky, *Aeneas, Sicily and Rome*, *Classical Philology* 66 (1971), 280–84.

T. Halter, *Vergil and Horaz*, *American Classical Review* 1 (1971), 209–10.

A. Richter, *Virgile, La huitième Bucolique*, *American Journal of Philology* 94 (1973), 207–9.

G. Binder, *Aeneas und Augustus*, *American Classical Review* 3 (1973), 15.

V. Buchheit, *Der Anspruch des Dichters in Vergils "Georgika,"* *Classical Philology* 71 (1976), 279–82.

W. Wimmel, *"Hirtenkrieg" und arkadisches Rom*, *Classical Philology* 71 (1976), 283–86.

P. Kragelund, *Dream and Prediction in the* Aeneid, *Classical World* 70 (1977), 482.

M. DiCesare, *The Altar and the City: A Reading of Vergil's* Aeneid, *Helios* 5 (1977), 78–82.

C. J. Fordyce, ed., *P. Vergili Maronis Aeneidos Libri VII–VIII*, *Vergilius* 24 (1978), 80–82.

S. Mack, *Patterns of Time in Vergil*, *Classical World* 73 (1979), 41.

P. Alpers, *The Singer of the* Eclogues, *Vergilius* 26 (1980), 74–77.

Ward W. Briggs, Jr., *Narrative and Simile from the* Georgics *in the* Aeneid, *Classical Outlook* 59 (1981–1982), 59.

R. D. Williams, ed., *Virgil: The Eclogues and* Georgics, *Vergilius* 27 (1981), 72–74.

P. A. Johnston, *Vergil's Agricultural Golden Age: A Study of the "Georgics,"* *Classical Philology* 77 (1982), 171–74.

Guy Lee, tr., *Virgil's Eclogues*, *Latomus* 41 (1982), 181–82.

L. P. Wilkinson, tr., *Virgil: The Georgics*, *Classical Outlook* 61 (1983–84), 69–70.

R. Wells, tr., *Virgil: The Georgics*, *Classical Outlook* 61 (1983–84), 69–70.

R. C. Monti, *The Dido Episode and the* Aeneid, *Classical Philology* 79 (1984), 72–76.

G. Williams, *Technique and Ideas in the* Aeneid, *American Journal of Philology* 105 (1984), 228–31.

R. Fitzgerald., tr., *The* Aeneid *of Virgil, Vergilius* 30 (1984), 64–67.

B. J. Bono, *Literary Transvaluation: From Vergilian Epic to Shakespearean Tragicomedy, Vergilius* 31 (1985), 85–87.

K. W. Gransden, *Virgil's* Iliad: *An Essay on Epic Narrative, Classical Outlook* 63 (1985), 33.

J. Griffin, *Latin Poets and Roman Life, Classical World* 80 (1987), 458–59.

G. B. Conte, *The Rhetoric of Imitation, American Journal of Philology* 108 (1987), 787–93.

J. D. Bernard, ed., *Vergil at 2000: Commemorative Essays on the Poet and his Influence, American Journal of Philology* 109 (1988), 267–70.

S. F. Wiltshire, *Public and Private in Vergil's* Aeneid, *Classical Outlook* 66 (1989), 99–100.

R. Thomas, ed., *Virgil: Georgics: Vol. 1, Books I–II; Vol. 2, Books III–IV, Classical Outlook* 67 (1989), 33.

D. O. Ross, Jr., *Virgil's Elements: Physics and Poetry in the* Georgics, *Classical Philology* 84 (1989) 349–54.

Annabel Patterson, *Pastoral and Ideology: Virgil to Valéry, Vergilius* 35 (1989), 133–37.

K. W. Gransden, *Virgil: The* Aeneid, *Classical World* 84 (1991), 477–78.

S. J. Harrison, ed., *Oxford Readings in Vergil's* Aeneid, *Classical Outlook* 69 (1991–92), 74–75.

David West, tr., *Virgil: The* Aeneid, *New England Classical Newsletter and Journal* 19 (1992), 41–42.

D. C. Feeney, *The Gods in Epic, New England Classical Newsletter and Journal* 20 (1993), 35–36.

R. J. Edgeworth, *The Colors of the* Aeneid, *Vergilius* 39 (1993), 69–73.

R. Heinze, *Virgil's Epic Technique* (trans. H. Harvey, D. Harvey, and F. Robertson), *Classical Journal* 90 (1994–95), 206–8.

M. O. Lee, *Virgil as Orpheus: A Study of the* Georgics, *Vergilius* 43 (1997), 127–31.

K. W. Gransden, ed., *Virgil in English, New England Classical Journal* 25 (1998), 103–4.

J. Wills, *Repetition in Latin Poetry: Figures of Allusion, American Journal of Philology* 119 (1998), 295–300.

M. Paschalis, *Virgil's* Aeneid: *Semantic Relations and Proper Names, Classical Journal* 94 (1998–99), 203–6.

R. A. Smith, *Poetic Allusion and Poetic Embrace in Ovid and Virgil, Religious Studies Review* 25 (1999), 93.

P. Hardie, *The Epic Successors of Virgil: A Study in the Dynamics of a Tradition, Arion* 6 (1999) 204–16.

A. J. Boyle, ed., *Roman Epic, Arion* 6 (1999), 204–16.

D. Hershkowitz, *The Madness of Epic: Reading Insanity from Homer to Statius, Journal of Roman Studies* 89 (1999), 220.

T. K. Hubbard, *The Pipes of Pan: Intertextuality and Literary Filiation in the Pastoral Tradition from Theocritus to Milton, Journal of Roman Studies* 90 (2000), 236–37.

L. Morgan, *Patterns of Redemption in Virgil's Georgics, Vergilius* 46 (2000), 155–62.

H. Heckel, *Das Widerspenstige zähmen. Die Funktion der militärischen und politischen Sprache in Vergils Georgica, Latomus* 61 (2002), 198–99.

J.-Y. Maleuve, *Violence et ironie dans les* Bucoliques *de Virgile, Latomus* 62 (2003),

176–78.

A. Rossi, *Contexts of War*: *Manipulation of Genre in Virgilian Battle Narrative*, *New England Classical Journal* 31 (2004), 322–27.

MISCELLANEOUS

"Virgil's *Aeneid*" (with J. Heffner and M. Hammond), *Classical World* 60 (1967), 377–88.

"Un Convegno Mondiale Scientifico di Studi su Vergilio," Vergilian Society Newsletter #29 (Fall 1981), 2–3 (= *The Georgia Classicist* 7 (1982), 1–3).

G. Highet, *Poets in a Landscape*, reprinted with a preface by Michael C. J. Putnam (New York: New York Review Books, 2010).

General Index

Index of Passages Cited